The Millennial Gentleman Handbook:
A Man's Guide to a Life of Etiquette, Prosperity and Good Fortune

By Carey Ray Martell

MillennialGentleman.com

The Millennial Gentleman Handbook
First Edition Printing, September 13th 2021
Copyright 2021 Carey R. Martell
　　All rights reserved.

ISBN-13: 9798476450061

Published by Martell Books (http://martellbooks.com/)

This book is dedicated to my brothers, in the hopes they may have a guidebook for teaching their own sons the things I tried to teach them as an older brother.

May the words in my book help young men grow to become Gentlemen of the Millennium.

Table of Contents

Introduction

In the modern generation, the breakdown of the traditional nuclear family has left many men with no positive male role models to show them the path to manhood and so they become adults without the collective wisdom of their male ancestors to guide them toward achieving success and prosperity in life. Although they are legally considered an adult, mentally many men today are still adolescents who spend a great deal of their time pursuing childish things and playing make believe, while rejecting reality. They can do this because we live in an artificial society that is quite different from the raw untamed natural world our ancestors lived in for millennia, where a person was primarily concerned with acquiring food for their next meal and did not have the free time for leisure like so many of us today do.

While humans are born as either a man or a woman biologically and this carries with it certain instinctive predispositions, in a cultural sense 'manhood' is a social identity role that is necessary for a functional human civilization in the same way that 'womanhood' is a necessary social identity role, too. This means both 'manhood' and 'womanhood' must be learned, and we cannot rely solely on our instincts to guide us. Our instincts were honed millennia ago by ancient ancestors who lived in a very different environment than the modern digital technology driven urban landscapes we have today. Our instincts were not shaped in an era where humans had to work a job for an employer and pay taxes, nor operate motor vehicles, or even concern themselves with avoiding overindulgence of the sugary foods widely available at a grocery store. These aspects of modern human civilization are things which necessitate education for a modern human to navigate, as our instincts are not designed to aid us in this kind of life. Our instincts are actually designed to assist humans with surviving in a harsh world of untamed nature, whose challenges necessitated all members of a human tribe to cooperate together. Each individual person had roles to perform they were best suited to, in order for the collective to survive and procreate. If this did not occur, the entire clan could perish.

Modern technology has eased the burden of survival on humans so that we have easier lives today, but we can still suffer misfortune if we fail to acknowledge those essential behaviors that lead to success for human communities throughout the ages; many of these behaviors remain essential regardless of the time period a person lives.

The great mistake that many postmodern philosophers make is to assume the world has been and always will be exactly the way it is at the moment the philosopher puts pen to paper. Their ideals are crafted in a vacuum of entitlement, separate from the harsh reality of life that rules most other people and this is the main reason why so many of these postmodern philosophies are fundamentally unworkable; when used for decision making, they often lead people to create their own misfortune.

How did our society get here? The answer is simple: war. The consequences of World War 1 resulted in the death of several generations of men all at once, and when the death toll is coupled with that of the Great Depression, the consequence is that many blood-lines of men were wiped out of existence, and with their deaths, generations of wealth both fiscal and of wisdom were lost, too. This lost wealth had been accumulating in many families for hundreds of years; some even a thousand. Now, suddenly, it was all gone as if it had never existed at all.

Then, humanity saw the rise of Socialism that led to Communism in parts of Western Europe and large parts of Asia. This, too, caused the mass extinction of generations of families and wealth. Massacres and famine as a consequence of poor social planning wiped them out. As Socialism was also a war on ideas, numerous libraries both private and public were burned to the ground – we don't even know what we have lost in the fires of Communism. No record exists anymore, for they were burned, too.

Then, World War 2 further destabilized the world. Once more, we saw bloodlines which had survived the aftermath of World War 1 wiped out. Worse, libraries around the world burned as the Axis sought to reshape the world in its own image. The villains failed, but in their deaths they took millions with them, too – not just the voices of those alive, but also the voices of those who had died in the past and tried to preserve their wisdom in the form of books.

So, what were the consequences of these events that took place in the 20th century? The result was that many generations of men grew up without fathers, and as father-less orphans they were not initiated into the rites of man-hood and taught how to be good productive members of a republic. Many men came of age not knowing how to teach their own sons how to be responsible men. The loss of male lives to war also led to many women entering the workforce; women took on roles in historically male dominated indus-tries, which led to mothers no longer staying at home to raise and educate the children. The states attempted to step in with the scaling of the public education system and estab-lishment of more schools, but they could ultimately not teach children everything that was necessary to be a gentle-man or a lady, and so the system has largely failed. Without mothers staying home with the children to ensure their de-velopment into functional stable adults, often kids are pushed into daycare centers and the school for the teaching of life skills. We now have many generations of adults in multiple age brackets who lack the skills and knowledge that was once ubiquitous in Western republics and allowed for them to be stable societies. This is all a great consequence of the World Wars and part of the long-term side effects they have wrought in society.

Stated plainly, many men today are becoming adults without having been initiated into the necessary cultural ritu-als that help them cement a strong identity as a man. They are born with fathers who are alive, but whom often do not teach them how to be a man. This is an exceptionally harder thing to teach in today's world, where misguided social ac-tivists pressure youth groups for boys to accept girls into them, which then forces what remains of the rituals of manhood to be toned down to accommodate the admission of girls. These men then, not having been properly initiated into manhood, have their own sons who are not raised into manhood, either, and so, so we have ended up with a widespread culture of boys who never grow up into ideal men and do not know how to teach other men how to be an ideal man.

This is problematic for these men because they are prone toward laziness; they lack enthusiasm for life and they lack ambition, often distracting themselves with activities that provide indulgence but do not demonstrably improve the quality of their lives in a measurable way, such as through the acquisition of wealth and the raising of functional, stable children. Indeed, many of these men choose to lock themselves away in a room to watch television and play video games with all their free hours; activities that allow the man to live vicariously through the adventures of fictional characters in a game that is designed to allow them to win and achieve much easier than it would be for them to do so in the real world. And because they do not know how to thrive in the society they exist in, they instead choose a superficial existence instead of spending the precious time of their lives toward more meaningful achievements. This can be regarded as a regressive identity, as the grown man is preferring playtime over achieving meaningful accomplishments with his life. This may benefit the multi-million-dollar game companies who create the games but it does not necessarily benefit the men who consume the games in far more abundance than they ought to. So many men today are absent of the achievements they otherwise might have accomplished in their lives if they had been raised in the rites of manhood.

Worst of all, many men fancy themselves to be intellectuals because they have attended some college or watched a few documentaries about a handful of things; yet, they have not read enough of the literature that drives the ideologies of the powerful influencers in the world today to understand what fuels the machinations of the global world. Without having read these books you are at a significant disadvantage and easily manipulated by more truly learned men. The back of this book features a 'Recommended Reading' section to guide men toward fixing this ignorance in their lives, but the amount of time that must be spent reading these books will take so much of your free time that the average man today may find it difficult to make the time to do so. Ideally, a boy would read these books sporadically over the normal course of his education while going from childhood to manhood but alas, few of these books are on required reading lists for grade school and high school courses. Only self-study in books can correct this neglect.

This brings us to the subject of why this book was written. In past generations it was traditional for a boy to be provided a book that provided advice for developing a productive social identity that will lead to success and prosperity in life once he became a man.

One of these genres is called Mirrors for princes. Mirrors for princes were popular for young nobles giving way to courtesy books and conduct books popular in the 18th century. These were common in many ancient cultures as well.

Unfortunately, these kinds of books for boys are no longer common today, to the detriment of young men. The few books that are printed today tend to offer advice that is outdated or poor. They generally do not instruct in virtues, which are those qualities of a person that define moral excellence. Without a good understanding of what is virtuous it becomes difficult to navigate good and evil moral choices in life. A prerequisite to living a virtuous life is to first have knowledge of that which is virtuous and why it is so.

In my time a cultural zeitgeist has moved against many of the ideals and virtues which I preach for in this book; that zeitgeist is called 'feminism'. To strive to become a gentleman now is to swim against a turbulent current that seeks to wash away all of the achievements and contributions of traditional manhood to society. The feminists seek to tarnish the memory and tear down the legacy of past great men who serve as the role models for generations of men and who epitomize the ideal of manhood. Yet, this is the path that you must traverse if you are to become a success in spite of the popularist movement against successful men that instead favors empty pleasures that lead to great misfortune and regrets. The advice I leave you in this book will guide you to success, but you must heed it and not deter from the path, regardless of what opposition may stand before you. The temptation to join a populist feminist circus is often great because it is easier to be swept up and flow along with a current than to swim against it. But I tell you that this populist movement against masculinity and manhood will throw you over a waterfall if you do not swim against it. Swim against it and achieve those great deeds that others cannot!

In the words of C.S. Lewis, 'When the whole world is running towards a cliff, he who is running in the opposite direction appears to have lost his mind.' Be wary of those who promise you a wholly happy life for all of your years, for it is not possible; choose instead a life of meaning, of heroism and a life of successful accomplishments. This latter is what I promise if you heed the words of my book.

This book will instruct you in cultivating qualities necessary for success in your life as a Man; ambition, self-reliance, self-improvement, honesty, and punctuality. It will also advise in your choice of friends and marriage, these too being necessary for your success in life.

This book encourages the institution of marriage and love. There are postmodernists who advocate for hedonistic lifestyles that discourage the bonding of two individuals in a deep, emotional, long-term joining of love and affection by advocating instead for shallow sexual relationships and shallow friendships formed largely through a digital portal controlled by corporations, such as social media companies or online video games.

Many postmodern ideologies also promote the idea that the purpose of individual life is to indulge into pleasurable diversions, especially those hobbies which produce revenue for corporations. This has become the norm at present,

8

and this commonplace hedonism is resulting in psychological conditioning in how people view relationships with others that prevents deep bonds from forming between individuals, even within those marriages which form today. Worse, the effects of this societal conditioning are encouraging a learned helplessness, causing many people to become extremely dependent upon the mob for guidance, but as this mob consists of those same hedonists who created the conditioning for learned helplessness to become so widespread. it is useless to turn to it for advice. If you turn to the mouths of madness for advice, the mouths will speak only madness back to you.

The potential of the masses becomes inhibited by the madness of the mobs, and so many who join these mad mobs are easily shackled by authoritarian despots who view the people only as a source of revenue and care nothing for what happens to them in their personal lives, nor how their learned helplessness destabilizes the society the despot seeks to rule, thus, it inches it closer to a societal collapse that does not benefit the despots own long term interests, either. History is full of examples of powerful and wealthy men whose achievements were rendered mute and their legacies lost within a generation or two due to such collapses.

Do not repeat their mistakes. If you are reading this book, you are among the bloodlines that have survived to present day against all odds. Do your best to keep it that away.

Reflecting on the state of the society I live in today, I would argue the modern Western civilized world has become a kind of dystopia.

As Aldous Huxley put it in 1961,

"There will be, in the next generation or so, a pharmacological method of making people love their servitude, and producing dictatorship without tears, so to speak, producing a kind of painless concentration camp for entire societies, so that people will in fact have their liberties taken away from them, but will rather enjoy it, because they will be distracted from any desire to rebel by propaganda or brainwashing, or brainwashing enhanced by pharmacological methods. And this seems to be the final revolution."

This book, *The Millennial Gentleman's Handbook*, is part of my effort to push back against societal destructive postmodern ideologies and encourage other men of my generation to do the same, before it is too late for anyone to prevent this final revolution from occurring.

Manhood is necessary for humanity's survival. That is why it exists. So, be excellent. Be a Man.

Carey Martell
September 4th, 2021

The Purpose of a Gentleman's Life

The ideal gentleman has a cool mind, a good voice that weaves beautiful, elegant and brave words, and demonstrates proper bearing and etiquette in his manner. He must also have a warrior spirit, athletic body and an excellent knowledge of the humanities, including art and history. The purpose of studying history is for imitation of that which is useful for good fortune, and avoidance of that which leads to misfortune. The sciences must also be learned, as well as the sociological ideas (which should not be construed as natural sciences) so that principles such as psychological operant conditioning may be used to your benefit and recognized when others seek to exploit these ideas to manipulate you for their own ends.

Many people believe the purpose of their life can be found in selfish pursuits, but this is not the way to finding meaningful purpose. The best way to think of yourself is by imagining the hand of your mother on your left shoulder, and the hand of your father on your right, as they both stand behind you. On each of their shoulders is also the hands of their own mothers and fathers, and so on with their great-grandparents, and on and on down your familial line to your earliest ancestors. You are connected deeply to the past in your very existence, the genes of your body are copies of those genes that were passed on to you down the ancestral

11

line and in you, a piece of them all continues to persist in this world; and their hands bolster you so that you can keep walking forward, if you only listen to them. And how does one listen to the embers of your ancestors still in you? By understanding what your instincts are driving you to do and how to wisely employ these drives to maximize the survival of the genetic legacy that was handed off to you and that you are tasked with handing on to your own children.

No man can live forever and no human has ever been supposed to. This is why a life spent focused on your own selfish pleasures will not lead to a life of contentment and lasting satisfaction. If you wish to obtain these qualities then you must take up the same duty as your past ancestors did, and make your guiding star the acquisition of generational wealth and the raising of a family to grow and safeguard these achievements. To recognize yourself as the inheritor of ancestral will and achievement, and do your own part to further this legacy. Making this your guiding principle will safeguard you from the path of hedonism more than any other practice can, for your priority will be your duty and what you serve more than it will be a fleeting happiness that is lost after the moment of pleasure has passed.

The word 'family' comes from the Latin 'familias' of Roman society. The paterfamilias, or father of the family, held the duty of administering the family with the intention of securing prosperity and furthering the reputation and legacy of his family. That is to say the purpose of a man in Roman society was to maintain and further his family's name in prestige. This is not unusual among early human societies and most all of them have a comparable concept as the familias and paterfamilias, which is why it is a useful model to use as a guide on how to live a prosperous life as a gentleman.

In the familias of Roman society the home estate was the symbol of the familias prosperity and legacy, as it would shelter its members through good and bad fortune in addition to serving as a rearing ground for the next generation of familias members. While the Romans bought and sold estates as much as people do in modern Western society, a familias always held a single family estate that was deeply associated with the history of the family, often decorated with relics and statues that marked important events in the familias legacy, and often included busts of the faces of the notable familias members. Through these artifacts young children would learn the importance of their family legacy and achievements, and be encouraged to earn their own place among the ancestors in the ancestral estate home.

Through the course of achieving accomplishments you will gain a degree of power, which can best be described as the ability to express it. Power is best viewed as the ability to influence others, and some degree of power is necessary for accomplishing goals that are beyond a single person to accomplish on their own. There are of course those who wield their power to do harm to others for the benefit of themselves and theirs, and the only way that they can be thwarted is through the wielding of power in return. This is because power can only be quelled by power; almost no one has ever obtained power that they have given up willingly. Therefore, the acquisition of some power is necessary to safeguard against becoming the victim of tyranny by others.

Civics education is necessary for all citizens for a functional republic to prosper. Republicanism, its roots and benefits, are not being taught effectively anymore which is making socialism more appealing to the masses, mistakenly so and to the detriment of human society.

Women have a special and necessary role in raising children in the values that lead to the children becoming adults who can themselves raise good children. This is something known to all human cultures through history, and which is preached in this book.

To end this part of the introduction, I leave you with the following phrase -- 'memento mori'. Remember you will die. Your duty as a boy is to grow into a man who will fulfil his duties as a man. The duty of all males in the human species is to pass on our genetic legacy and valuable gene adaptations we gain during our lifetime to our children so that they will inherit our strengths and be that much more prepared for succeeding in life.

In my generation, corporations have heavily promoted the idea of focusing entirely on personal indulgence over familial duty because these corporations wish for individual men and women to spend money on their services and products which are indulgences. Some even encourage the idea of not having children at all so that a person can focus more of their money on giving themselves these indulgences. Be cautious about building your personal identity based on the advertising campaigns of multimillion dollar enterprises that profit others, as typically these people will lead you astray for their own benefit and not for yours. They only want you to purchase their products and they do not care about your long-term success nor that of your family. It is your responsibility to be wise enough to not succumb to their clever words and drift away from the time-tested proven model for how a young man should live his life to ensure the prosperity for himself and his family. This book is designed to help you navigate this path.

I hope the essays of this book help you live an exciting life of elegance and adventure.

Virtues and the Code of Chivalry for a Modern Gentleman

I often mention virtues and chivalry for a modern gentleman, but it occurs to me that I have yet to expressly discuss
the topic of what virtues and a code of chivalry is. As many
people are under the erroneous impression that chivalry is
only a set of rules for how a man treats a woman it is probably worth being more clear on what is meant when I refer to
such things.

I am an atheist. I was raised as a Lutheran but have
abandoned superstitious ways of thinking about the world
and my place within it in favor of a more objective, scientifi-
cally based one. Yet I still find value in these traditional
ideas such as virtues and codes of chivalry, as I respect and
acknowledge what these ideas produce in society is good for
all. As atheism is not a moral philosophy in and of itself, I
have needed to construct my own ethical code. After spending many years studying all major religions and looking for
common threads between them I developed what I refer to
as 'Chivalric Humanism'. It is a philosophical code by
which I live my life in accordance with traditional ideas
through a lens of Humanist ideals. I believe my code is a rel-

evant moral compass for the modern world and can be of assistance to others, which is why I am sharing it here in this article.

What is Chivalry and Virtues?

Historically, the code of chivalry is a code of conduct followed by knights. Chivalry was an informal code practiced among historical knights, with some codes specifically tied to certain knightly orders. The specific codes each order followed sometimes differed between these groups of knights. For example, *The Latin Rule*, a document of 72 clauses, outlined the regulations and prescribed the etiquette for members of the Knights Templars. Most codes of chivalry were very similar to each other and covered the same general ideas of what constituted honorable and noble behavior. Over generations as the social class of knight declined in influence these chivalrous ideals became the code of the remaining classes of nobility and trickle downed to lower social classes as the concept of a gentleman took shape.

Yet virtues are universal concepts appearing in every human culture. There are the well-known cardinal virtues of Platonic thought, and the later seven heavenly virtues of Catholic Christianity that heavily influenced concepts of chivalry for European knights and stood in contrast to the seven deadly sins. Virtues even appear within other non-European cultures; there is for example the Eightfold Path of Buddhism and Confucianism also has a set of virtues, too. Every human culture has a set list of virtues that developed and date back to ancient human history; the periods of early civilization and tribalism.

Because the names we prescribe to virtues are labels of our own invention, many people dismiss these as nothing but noble lies; yet these concepts are universal to humans, appearing in every culture. My explanation for this occurrence is that humans naturally come up with labels for these qualities because our instincts tell us that these virtues define the quality of that which is 'good', for these are the personal qualities that made our ancestors' tribes safer and more stable. The prosperity that many generations of humans gained when the members of their communities abided by these qualities have left us with an inherited genetic memory — that which we call 'instinct'. This is not to suggest that our instincts are always correct but rather that those qualities which have allowed humans to build prosperous civilizations are essentially 'good' to us at an instinctual level. Our instincts do require us to learn good teachings in order to decipher correctly how to interpret our instincts, especially when we find ourselves in situations our ancestors never had to deal with (which many people encounter today on a daily basis in the modern world). In these new situations sometimes our instincts can be mistaken and that is why codes such as chivalry are so very useful; these codes seek to provide people with rules for how to behave in difficult situations that might trigger instincts that are not helpful (faults) while encouraging us toward instincts that are useful (virtues) for the present circumstances of the world we live in.

The code that I have devised for my own life path is what I call Chivalric Humanism. It is intended to be a universal code of chivalry that anyone can subscribe to regardless of any other religious upbringing as it is not religion specific. I as an atheist designed it to be useful to myself and conform to the values I was taught as a child, which are those values which have been useful for me to acquire the success I have in life. Because I have strived to live my life by this code of my own making I have often found that people have given me aid when I had no entitlement to it, and these instances have made all the difference in times of crisis in my life. Yet I cannot promise you that everyone will cooperate with you just because you follow my code, for just as many people have turned their back on me when I would not be a participant to their evil.

What I can promise you is that I can live my life without any shame, guilt or regret from mistakes when I follow this code in my decision making, and when I start to stray from right action it is this code which brings me back to the proper path of chivalry. If you use this code as a compass to navigate your life you are unlikely to do evil and make the world a darker place than it already is; if anything, if you follow this code you have a higher chance of making it a brighter one for the people whose lives you impact.

Why Are Codes of Chivalry Still Needed?

In order to understand how to improve ourselves we must be able to identify those aspects of our personality we can improve, but before even this we have to identify what are good and negative qualities in a person. This is the purpose of virtues. Virtues serve as some of the most important of rules for people; these rules being necessary because attempting to calculate the consequences of actions during the moment one needs to make decisions will frequently result in a person making hasty decisions that result in less than optimal courses of action being pursued. In summary it is difficult to remember the many specific rules of etiquette a person should abide by in order to be a good person, so simpler codes of conduct based around virtuous concepts developed.

Rather than memorizing hundreds of rules a person instead follows the principles of virtues that describe the type of character a person should strive for. The individual then has a very flexible rule structure that can accommodate many different kinds of scenarios. Essentially, by focusing on being a good person then the right actions will follow.

In this world people live their lives following many different ideals. The freedom for one to choose how they wish to live their life is a blessing, yet this freedom can often make it difficult to distinguish what moral qualities separate the good from the evil, and the righteous from the false. It is of my opinion that it is virtues that are the moral characteristics which distinguish respectable people from wicked folk. It is because of virtues that a society of people are able to live together peacefully, while those without virtue live in constant disdain and discomfort while labeled as violators of social contracts, and are distrusted.

Without even a code of conduct to follow people cannot maintain their relationships with each other and without these relationships the fabric of a society weakens. In order for society to grow and prosper all people must therefore grant each other a common base of consideration. The foundation for this mutual respect are the virtues, and although one person might gain a personal and temporary advantage by behaving unvirtuous, society as a whole will ultimately suffer when many people engage in these violations. Thus it is that when you advance yourself in virtue you also help advance humanity by performing acts that benefit humanity as a whole. It is only those who are willing to face their own faults and try to overcome them that will grow and gain the fruits of their labor.

It is not enough to simply read a blog post to acquire virtue, as true virtue is gained through experience and develops as a kind of skill to employ to right action. Yet it is still important that one study the principles and virtues here in order to understand what the virtues are defined as. A virtuous character is developed through habit; if you do the correct things again and again, eventually it will become part of your character to act in this way as a habit.

Four Positive Principles and Eight Virtues in Chivalric Humanism

In order to understand how to improve ourselves we must be able to identify those aspects of our personality we can improve, but before even this we have to identify what are positive and negative qualities in a person. This is the purpose of virtues. Virtues serve as some of the most important rules for Chivalric Humanists; these rules being necessary because attempting to calculate the consequences of actions during the moment one needs to make decisions will frequently result in a person making hasty decisions that result in less than optimal courses of action being pursued. In summary it is difficult to remember the many rules of proper conduct a person should abide by in order to be a good person.

By instead following the principles of virtues that describe the type of character a person should strive for, an individual will have a very flexible rule structure that can accommodate many different kinds of scenarios. Essentially, by focusing on being a good person then the right actions will follow.

This I believe is one of the great strengths of a virtue-based moral framework; many postmodern philosophies have a tendency to become convoluted as the philosopher who originated the ideas becomes more focused in solving philosophical problems than in creating a useful framework that can be employed by the average person in their daily life. Complicated frameworks with many special rules break down when attempted in realistic situations that subject a person to mental stress and unexpected obstacles. Virtues are more flexible as guideposts for behavior as even when a person is stressed and becomes prone to emotional thinking they can recall what virtuous behavior is. Past generations of humans understood this, and so the most learned of philosophers employed their best reasonings to construct moral frameworks based around virtues which could then be learned and used to guide behavior by the average person who may not necessarily understand the logic behind the virtues.

In this world people live their lives following many different ideals. The freedom for one to choose how they wish to live their life is a blessing, yet this freedom can often make it difficult to distinguish what moral qualities separate the good from the evil, and the righteous from the false. In my opinion, it is virtues that are the moral characteristics which distinguish respectable people from wicked folk. It is because of virtues that a society of people are able to live together peacefully, while those without virtue live in constant disdain and discomfort while labeled as violators of social contracts, and are then distrusted.

Without even a code of conduct to follow people cannot maintain their relationships with each other and without these relationships the fabric of a society weakens. In order for society to grow and prosper all people must therefore grant each other a common base of consideration. The foundation for this mutual respect are the virtues, and although one person might gain a personal and temporary advantage by behaving unvirtuous, society as a whole will ultimately suffer when many people engage in these violations. Thus it is that when you advance yourself in virtue you also help advance humanity by performing acts that benefit humanity. It is only those who are willing to face their own faults and try to overcome them that will gain the fruits of their labor.

There are some people who construct their identity from external accomplishments which are subject to whimsical change, such as their relationships to others, occupations, social status, and possessions. When the foundations of a person's identity is built upon these external things and events, it leads a person to be anxious and fearful of losing the factors that define their identities. While a person should cultivate positive relationships, seek success in their careers and possess good resources, a person cannot keep the world frozen in place so that these things are always present in their lives. This means anxiety will always be a persistent thorn in their minds as they fear their world becoming undone when change inevitably occurs and they lose these external things in their life. Anxiety is to be diminished in life as much as possible, as anxiety leads to psychosis; a madness of the mind.

Instead of building an identity based on external factors such as relationships (with lovers, parents, children and friends) or possessions, a person should instead base their self-value on the cultivation of virtues, qualities and other personal capacities. This provides a more solid foundation for a personal identity. It is designed that through the walking on the road of Chivalric humanism a person will cultivate these qualities and in so doing, also develop associated skills the person can use throughout their life to adapt to changing circumstances and environments they find themselves in when change inevitably occurs; these new acquired skills also have the added benefit of helping a person better achieve their full potential as a person as well.

When living a life rooted in virtue, personal identity then becomes anchored to values a person chooses rather than tied to external things one cannot always control. A person then lives a purposeful life when living a life defined by virtues, with a mind that is strong.

The virtues of Chivalric Humanism are not brand-new ideas; they are the values of past generations of humans that have been handed down to us as culture. This section will include several quotes from noteworthy humans throughout history that reflect the universality of these ideas, so that you may understand these virtues better. The first quote, that reflects the prior passage I wrote, is this one;

> *"Not being able to govern events, I govern myself. If they will not adapt to me, I adapt to them."*
> –Lord Michel de Montaigne, 16th century French philosopher and Lord of Montaigne

While it is not enough to simply read a book to acquire virtue and that true virtue is gained through experience as a kind of skill to employ to act rightly in the correct situation, it is still important that one study the principles and virtues here in order to understand what the virtues are defined as.

A virtuous character is developed through habit; if you do the correct things again and again, eventually it will become part of your character to act in this way in daily life.

The Four Positive Principles

In my experience, there are "Four Positive Principles" that serve as the building blocks of right action.

These Principles are: *Truth*, *Love*, *Courage* and *Wisdom*. Although one may have an infinite number of reasons to perform a positive action, such as those driven by charity or pity, one or some of the Four Principles will stand out as deciding factors in these decisions.

The Principles are;

Truth:
The quality of acting in accordance with fact or reality.

Love:
The quality of having an intense feeling of deep affection.

Courage:
The quality of a confident character who is not afraid or intimidated easily but without being incautious or inconsiderate.

Wisdom.
The quality of having experience, knowledge, and good judgment

All of the virtues can be built from these Four Positive Principles, and they can be combined in eight ways, which I call the "Eight Noble Virtues". The Eight Noble Virtues are that which those who strive to build a peaceful and honorable society should erect their moral foundation upon.

Thus, from the possibilities which spawned the Four Positive Principles of Truth, Love Courage and Wisdom come the Eight Noble Virtues of Loyalty, Altruism, Valor, Respect, Hope, Humility, Integrity and Duty.

The Eight Noble Virtues

1. Loyalty: *Be faithful to your family, your friends, and your community.*

The Principles of Truth and Love becomes *Loyalty*, for without honesty between people, how can we build the trust which is needed to maximize our successes?

Loyalty also flows from love. Love nurtures trust among people, creating bonds of friendship. Genuine loyalty is then only created after sharing hardships together, causing the bond to overflow with love and compassion. As long as there are bonds like this then communities shall not descend into evil. By contrast, power that is unrestricted by bonds will often bring about great calamities.

Being faithful is a matter of believing in and devoting yourself to something or someone. A loyal Chivalric humanist is one who supports the leadership and stands up for their fellows.

Likewise, you should be loyal to your family and friends. You should be honest about your intentions with them, and remember that loyal service means telling hard truths. If they need assistance with some problem and are capable of helping, you demonstrate loyalty by doing so. Loyalty isn't grey; it is black or white. You can't be loyal only when it suits you. You are either completely loyal or not loyal at all.

"The scholar does not consider gold and jade to be precious treasures, but instead loyalty and good faith."
–Confucius, 5th century BCE Chinese philosopher

2. Altruism: *Be concerned for the suffering and misfortunes of others.*

The Principles of Love and Wisdom becomes *Altruism* or selflessness, for at some time or another all of us will need to rely on the kindness of others, and compassion is most likely to be shown to those who have exhibited it themselves.

A benevolent person is ever mindful of those who are suffering and in distress. Beginning with empathy for others in distress, benevolence can be described as the correct use of your power to act for the good of the recipient. One must always be generous in so far as your resources allow; this unselfishness counters gluttony. It also makes the path of mercy easier to discern when a difficult decision of justice is required.

Altruism should not be confused for over-indulgence of another's vices; providing alcohol and drugs to an addict does not make a person compassionate as this act is not a correct use of your resources for the good of the addict. The altruistic act would be to encourage someone to overcome their addictions with support.

Selfless service is an aspect of altruism. Selfless service is larger than just one person. In serving your community, you are doing your duty loyally without requiring recognition or gain. The basic building block of selfless service is the commitment of each team member to go a little further, endure a little longer, and look a little closer to see how he or she can add to the effort.

A Chivalric humanist should hold with conviction that with reason, an open exchange of ideas, good-will, and tolerance that progress can be made in building a better world for ourselves and others.

"Service to others is the rent you pay for your room here on earth."
–Muhammad Ali, 20th century American boxer

"In the long history of the world, only a few generations have been granted the role of defending freedom in its hour of maximum danger. I do not shrink from this responsibility - I welcome it."
-John F. Kennedy, 35th President of the United States

3. Valor: *Be without fear in the face of adversity.*

The <u>Principles of Courage and Wisdom</u> becomes *Valor*, for without valor people will never reach into the unknown or dare to tempt fate, and thus will never achieve their accomplishments.

Valor is not simply courage, but that strength of mind in regard to danger; that quality which enables a person to encounter danger with firmness, personal bravery, prowess and intrepidity. Valor carries a connotation of self-sacrifice in that you are being brave despite knowing you may fail but you are aware that it is more important that you try anyway.

Valor has long been associated with knighthood. With physical courage, it is a matter of enduring physical duress and at times risking personal safety. Facing moral fear or adversity may be a long, slow process of continuing forward on the right path, especially if taking those actions is not popular with others. You can build your personal courage by daily standing up for and acting upon the things that you know are honorable.

Now then, let us consider what is the difference between a hero and a coward? There isn't much difference; inside they are alike. Both a hero and a coward can become afraid; they both fear dying and getting hurt. The difference between a hero and a coward is that what a hero does makes him a hero, and it is what the other doesn't do that makes him a coward. There is no one who can know courage who has not first known fear. Yet it is weak to yield to fear and heroic to face danger without flinching. A coward runs away, while a hero steps forward. Our actions decide what side of the line we fall on.

True courage is found not only in facing death, but also in facing losing, ridicule or even admitting when one is in the wrong. True courage, then, is never allowing your desires to cause you to sacrifice the smallest amount of your honor to win through cheating, and to accept an honorable, if disappointing, defeat rather than take a glorious, but tainted victory.

It is expected that a Chivalric humanist has the compassion to not be a bully and the courage to not be a bystander.

"There are risks and costs to action. But they are far less than the long range risks of comfortable inaction."
–John F. Kennedy, 35th President of the United States

"Have the courage to say no. Have the courage to face the truth. Do the right thing because it is right. These are the magic keys to living your life with integrity."
–W. Clement Stone, 20th century businessman and philanthropist

"Courage is what preserves our liberty, safety, life and our homes and our parents; our country and children. Courage comprises all things."
– Titus Maccius Plautus, 2nd century BCE Roman playwright

"The secret of happiness is freedom, and the secret of freedom, courage."
--Thucydides, 4th century BCE Athenian philosopher and historian

4. **Respect:** *Treat others with dignity and courtesy while expecting others to do the same.*

The <u>Principle of Love</u> and the <u>Principle of Courage</u> give us *Respect*, for people who care for each other will be willing to make personal sacrifices to help each other in need. Deeds which one day you may need returned to you, or which surpass our own needs because they serve a greater purpose.

Respect is what allows us to appreciate the best in other people. Respect allows us to acknowledge the inherent value in other people and their worth. Respect is trusting that people have done their jobs and fulfilled their duty when you have no cause to believe otherwise. And self-respect results from knowing you have put forth your best effort. Respect is knowing that within a group each of us has something to contribute.

Respect is also having a tempered attitude towards the usage of resources, whether natural occurring or man-made. To be wasteful of resources is a disservice to others who also need access to those items, and shows them disrespect.

Respect is also benevolence of the strong toward the weak. Bullying is not appropriate and has no place in the civilized world. Not everyone can walk at the same pace as another, and needs to be supported on how to become stronger. Respect also requires breaking a hard truth gracefully to someone and offering criticism to others in a way that is constructive rather than spirit crushing. Your measure as a moral person can be determined by how you treat those who can do nothing for or against you.

Acts of courtesy should be the result of your consideration for the feelings of others. It should not be a result of fear of offending good taste or convention. The more it is practiced, the greater becomes your consideration for others and your understanding of other people's points of view.

There are two great threats to courtesy. These are thoughtlessness and one's reaction to discourtesy, real or perceived. Guard well against making speech without prior thought to the impact of your words on others, for it is far too easy to give offense with a careless word. This is not a difficult problem to overcome; it takes only a little consideration for others. The true test of courtesy comes in attempting courtesy in the face of discourtesy. Remember that someone else's poor behavior is no reason for you to respond in kind. To do so would only reduce your own virtue.

Try to see instances of discourtesy, rather than as an attack to be angered by, instead as an opportunity to test and show your virtue. He who successfully shows grace under pressure of courtesy in the face of discourtesy is truly honorable.

"It's easy to do anything in victory. It's in defeat that a man reveals himself."
– Floyd Patterson, 20th century American boxer

"I speak to everyone in the same way, whether he is the garbage man or the president of the university."
– Albert Einstein, 20th century scientist

5. Hope: *Possess an optimistic attitude, no matter the challenges you face.*

By combining the <u>Principles of Truth, Love and Courage,</u> the virtue of *Hope* is created; the virtue that causes one to possess an optimistic attitude, no matter the challenges you face.

Hope, sometimes also known as perseverance, is the moral strength which enables people to endure the hardships they encounter, never allowing themselves to be sidetracked from success. Perseverance is the skeleton key to all kinds of success in life.

To be hopeful is to be determined to accomplish your goals regardless of obstacles. It is to seek excellence in all endeavors you undertake, not just those regarding your duties in your daily job. It is also to seek out strength to be used in the service of the greater good, rather than to be used merely for personal gain.

Hope is also to be self-reliant. Do not wait for someone else to do your job for you. Do not wait for the things you want in the world to be handed to you on a platter. This does not mean that you have to do something completely alone if you have no idea how to do it, or if you cannot do it. What it does mean is that you should learn things from life; learn how to solve common problems, and maybe learn a craft or two. Study books of knowledge so you can learn all you can about the world to help you in the future when that information may become incredibly vital to the survival of you or someone else.

A hopeful person will remain firm in the belief that things will get better. You should believe that collectively the human capacity for goodness will always overcome the capacity for evil. If we lose faith in this then we no longer have the grounds for hope.

It is a Chivalric Humanist's duty to be a strong pillar in times of tragedy. Hope is the shining armour that shields a person from despair and inspires others to follow suit.

"Hope is being able to see that there is light despite all of the darkness."
– Desmond Tutu, 20th century South African cleric and humanitarian

"Courage is like love: it must have hope for nourishment."
– Napoleon Bonaparte, 18th century military general and Emperor of France

6: Humility: *To recognize and accept your own shortcomings with grace.*

The sixth Virtue is *Humility,* which flows from the Principles of Truth and Wisdom. To be humble is to safeguard against being prideful, which leads to arrogance, which causes one to disregard the consequences that one's actions have on other people.

Because humility is not flashy and requires a person to accept things they may not enjoy about themselves, as a virtue it is often overlooked but no other virtue is of any assistance when you must hold-fast against vanity. Although we can never completely eliminate our inherent capacity for vanity we can hold it at bay by wielding humility with sincerity. When practiced with sincerity, humility refuses the comforts of praise, keeps you listening to the quiet whisperings of truth and confers a measure of grace.

Sincerity is the key to humility. Humility that is play-acted, even if you yourself are the audience, is powerless; indeed, it becomes a weapon of vainglory rather than being used against it. To seek sincerity requires the onerous duty of peering inside you to see both the light and the darkness; the good and the bad, the excellent and the poor. To accept these things as truths is a daunting, yet noble task. Once the truth is seen, one has the further duty to seek to improve those virtues in which he is lacking. It is the attempt to work towards the ideal of humility that makes one humble; there will never be one who reaches the ideal, and yet this virtue may be gained even though the ideal itself remains unreachable.

How is this accomplished? By avoiding the comfort awarded by praise. Should you strive to behave honorably, you will in due course earn honor and praise from those who see you as virtuous. And yet you must avoid placing too much weight on this praise, even if it is purchased on the authority of your own integrity. Vanity is too clever for that; it can easily overtake you. As soon as you are comfortable that you are a virtuous person who has acted with righteousness, you are as vulnerable as a babe to vanity's jaded charms.

"It is unwise to be too sure of one's own wisdom. It is healthy to be reminded that the strongest might weaken and the wisest might err."
– Mahatma Gandhi, 20th century Indian lawyer and social activist

"On the highest throne in the world, we still sit only on our own bottom."
– Michel de Montaigne, 16th century philosopher

"Do not seek after the sages of the past. Seek what they sought."
– Matsuo Bashō, 17th century Japanese poet

7. Integrity: *Do what is right, morally and legally.*

By combining the <u>Principles of Truth, Wisdom and Courage</u> we find the virtue of Integrity.

Integrity is a quality you develop by adhering to moral principles. It requires that you do and say nothing that deceives those who have your trust, and defend the weak and the helpless from oppression. When actions do not follow words, there can be little trust. As your integrity grows, so does the trust others place in you. The more choices you make based on integrity, the more this highly prized value will affect your relationships with family and friends, and, finally, the fundamental acceptance of yourself.

A Chivalric humanist should have an interest in securing justice and fairness in society and in eliminating unjust discrimination and intolerance. You must possess a sense of stewardship of humanity's future and unfeigned love for people. A person should be as good as his word and a handshake.

It is to be mentioned that deception has a place in warfare and other situations where lives may be at risk. It is necessary for a military commander to achieve strategic and tactical advantages through surprise in order to serve the greater good of achieving victory. It is critical to remember that the positive principle of 'Truth' in Chivalric Humanism means to act in accordance with reality and this also means to always consider the circumstances a person finds themselves in. In private conduct one never has permission to be deceptive between those of good faith, but in matters of life and death against an enemy who wishes to do harm, some amount of deception is permissible in order to serve goodness. The ultimate aim of war is to achieve peace, and this must be remembered, else a person act in a way that is inconsistent to the reality of the situation they are in.

"When I tell the truth, it is not for the sake of convincing those who do not know it, but for the sake of defending those that do."
– William Blake, 19th century poet and painter

"The first thing is to be honest with yourself. You can never have an impact on society if you have not changed yourself. Great peacemakers are all people of integrity, of honesty, but humility."
— Nelson Mandela, 1st President of Republic of South Africa after apartheid ended

8. Duty: *Fulfil your obligations to humanity.*

Duty stems from all of the Principles; Wisdom because it requires a person to carefully consider the consequences of their actions; Courage because serving often requires a person to stand against doubts and fears; Truth because Duty must always be guided by it; and Love for humankind.

Based on the social contract you have with superiors such as teachers and managers, it is your duty to obey their instructions, but doing your duty means more than carrying out your assigned tasks. Duty means being able to accomplish tasks as part of a team. You fulfill your obligations as a part of your team every time you resist the temptation to take "shortcuts" that might undermine the integrity of the final product of the team.

A person should have an interest in securing justice and fairness in society and in eliminating unjust discrimination and intolerance. You must also possess a sense of stewardship of humanity's future and unfeigned love for people.

Furthermore, as a Chivalric humanist you should have a commitment to the use of critical reason, factual evidence and scientific method of inquiry in seeking solutions to problems and answers to important questions. You should be committed to making your life meaningful through better understanding of human history, intellectual and artistic achievements, and the outlooks of those who differ from yourself. You should be concerned with the fulfillment, growth and creativity of both individual people and humankind in general.

"Not for ourselves alone are we born."
– Marcus Tullius Cicero, 1st century BCE Roman statesman and philosopher

"Bad men need nothing more to compass their ends, than that good men should look on and do nothing."
– John Stuart Mill, 19th century philosopher and English statesman

"What matters is the countless small deeds of unknown people, who lay the basis for the significant events that enter history."
– Howard Zinn, 20th century American historian

In Conclusion about Virtues

A person who lives by these core values is an honorable person. Honor is essentially the combined traits of a person who follows the Eight Virtues. Honor is what is achieved by living up to the ideals and pursuing the qualities and behavior listed above.

The honor of a Chivalric humanist is a sacred thing to the self and cannot be lightly set aside or trampled on. A person develops the habit of being honorable through deeds and solidifies that habit with every value choice they make. Honor is a matter of carrying out, acting, and living the values of Loyalty, Altruism, Valor, Respect, Hope, Humility, Integrity and Duty in everything you do. Therefore, the Virtues are designed to be utilized as a collective to guide decision making, and they should not be used in isolation. They each have a role in decision making, especially regarding the most complicated issues.

"A moral change still depends on the individual and not on the passage of any law."
– Eleanor Roosevelt, Former First Lady of the United States

"This is a subtle truth. Whatever you love, you are."
– Jalal ad-Din Muhammad Rumi, 13th century Persian poet

The Four Negative Principles and Eight Faults

"An evil cause produces an evil effect; Sow evil and reap evil."
— Buddhist proverb

Just as there are positive principles and virtues, there are the opposite. These are the Four Negative Principles and Eight Faults.

The Eight Faults are the shadows of the Eight Virtues, for they are corrupted versions of the Virtues. They are those qualities which, left unchecked and opposed in the heart, set a person on a path toward evil. As the Eight Virtues are built from the Positive Principles, the Faults are built from negative principles.

The Four Negative Principles are the antithesis to the Four Positive Principles:

The *Negative Principle of Falsehood* is opposite to the Positive Principle of Truth.

Falsehood is the quality of fabricating information to appear true. Falsehood obscures truth and makes it difficult to make objective decisions.

The *Negative Principle of Hatred* is opposite to the Positive Principle of Love.

Hatred is an intense dislike for someone or something. While it is always necessary to stand firmly against evil things, a person must not succumb to hatred because it blinds us from objectivity and encourages us to do harm that has no good purpose.

The *Negative Principle of Cowardice* is opposite to the Positive Principle of Courage.

Cowardice is different from Fear. Fear is natural and sometimes useful; but cowardice is to give in to fear at the expense of what is known to be morally right because you are unwilling to become courageous.

The *Negative Principle of Ignorance* is opposite to the Positive Principle of Wisdom.

Ignorance is the state of lacking knowledge. While all people are born ignorant, part of the noble purpose of life is to overcome ignorance through the pursuit of wisdom.

The Eight Faults

The Eight Faults are the opposite of the Eight Noble Virtues. They are faults, not vices, because it is normal that humans can make mistakes. By acknowledging these faults in our thoughts and actions we can learn to realize our drawbacks and then work to improve those aspects of ourselves which are in need of bolstering, transforming a fault within ourselves into a virtue.

The <u>Negative Principle of Falsehood and Hatred</u> becomes the <u>Fault of Treachery</u>, the anti-Loyalty. Treachery leads people to betray their friends and family so they can be oppressed for the benefit of the traitor. Betrayal is the breaking or violation of a contract, trust, or confidence. Treachery is the opposite of Loyalty and creates conflict within a relationship amongst individuals, between organizations or between individuals and organizations.

> *"He who throws away a friend is as bad as he who throws away his life."*
> —Sophocles, 4th century BCE Greek playwright

The <u>Negative Principles of Ignorance and Hatred</u> becomes the <u>Fault of Selfishness</u>, the anti-Altruism. Selfishness is being concerned excessively or exclusively, for oneself or one's own advantage, pleasure, or welfare, regardless of others. Selfishness often leads to cruel behavior, such as to enjoy causing the pain and suffering of others. When one hates and is narcissistic they often begin to think pleasantly of any manner of ill omen coming upon their enemies and this masochism is cruelty. Selfishness is based on ignorance of how a person should act for the benefit of humankind.

> *"Every man must decide whether he will walk in the light of creative altruism or in the darkness of destructive selfishness."*
> —Martin Luther King Jr, 20th century preacher and social activist.

The <u>Negative Principles of Ignorance and Cowardice</u> becomes the <u>Fault of Greed,</u> for those who live in fear desire power in order to compensate for their perceived insufficiencies stemming from their fears. Yet Greed is built on ignorance because power cannot compensate for personal defects of character.

Greed often leads a person to become loathsome, which is a contempt of others for the perceived advantages they have while we perceive ourselves as being less fortunate. Loathing is a form of self-pity, despicable and cowardly. An attempt to tear down others fortunes because of our misfortunes and attempt to make them suffer because we suffer. This is a terrible thing to do.

> *"So, the unwanting soul sees what's hidden, and the ever-wanting soul sees only what it wants."*
> –Lao Tzu, 4th century BCE Chinese philosopher

The <u>Negative Principles of Hatred and Cowardice</u> become the <u>Fault of Disrespect,</u> which makes a person disregard the affairs of anyone else, even if they are loyal to you. If you make no attempt to respect others they will not attempt to respect you for you have shown hostilities toward them which they find uncivil. Disrespect results in unnecessary fights to occur, which may result in either parties suffering, or even resulting in untimely death of the participants. Thus it is that to disrespect others is to invite conflict.

"Rudeness is the weak man's imitation of strength."
–Eric Hoffer, 20th century American philosopher

The <u>Negative Principles of Cowardice, Hatred and False-hood</u> become the <u>Fault of Despair</u>, which is born from the death of Hope. Despair is very self-destructive and can lead to self-doubt and hesitation when faced with important matters that result in tragedies for ourselves and others. To not act because we are afraid yet lie to ourselves about being afraid, this is what despair is. Despair can even cause a person to lose the will to live.

"If you are distressed by anything external, the pain is not due to the thing itself, but to your estimate of it; and this you have the power to revoke at any moment."
–Marcus Aurelius, 1st century Roman Emperor and philosopher

The <u>Negative Principles of Falsehood and Ignorance</u> is the <u>Fault of Vanity</u>, which brings about arrogance and the delusion that others are not as worthy of comforts and happiness as you. If you cannot look at others as being equally worthy of courtesy and value then you will not treat them properly as they should be treated and thus will disrespect them. This is to be conceited, the opposite of Humility.

"Vanity and pride are different things, though the words are often used synonymously. A person may be proud without being vain. Pride relates more to our opinion of ourselves, vanity to what we would have others think of us."
– Jane Austen, 19th century English novelist

The <u>Negative Principles of Falsehood, Ignorance, and Cowardice</u> creates the <u>Fault of Dishonesty</u>, which is the opposite of Integrity and caused by intentional spreading of a Falsehood. Dishonesty is born from fears that one cannot succeed in goals through honest means. Sometimes we are also dishonest with ourselves and fabricate a belief as a means to avoid confronting a disappointing truth.

"Whoever is detected in a shameful fraud is ever after not believed even if they speak the truth."
–Plato, 3rd century BCE Athenian philosopher

Lastly, the <u>Fault of Recklessness</u> is the opposite of Duty, and stems from all of the Negative Principles: Ignorance for it is based in not thinking carefully about the consequences of one's actions; Falsehood because reckless actions ignore the reality of circumstances surrounding a situation; Cowardice because it is fear that drives a person to reckless action; and Hatred because it is anger that guides the reckless mind.

The Fault of Recklessness causes a person to be irresponsible and incapable of performing Duty on behalf of humankind.

*"There are five dangerous faults which may affect a
general:
(1) Recklessness, which leads to destruction;
(2) cowardice, which leads to capture;
(3) a hasty temper, which can be provoked by insults;
(4) a delicacy of honor which is sensitive to shame;
(5) over-solicitude for his men, which exposes him to worry
and trouble."*
– Sun Tzu, 5th century BCE Chinese general and author of
The Art of War

In Conclusion About Faults:

It is important to acknowledge that Virtues and
Faults are found in all people, and they are the building
blocks of our personality. As such a single individual may
possess a mixture of these qualities at any one time that
shapes their personality at the present moment.

It is critical to know that when you recognize a Fault
in yourself you must work diligently to undo the cause of
that Fault, which is by restraining the negative principles
that created the Fault in the first place. Strive instead to do
good by adhering to the principles of its opposite Virtue.
Embracing a Virtue within your heart will restrain its corre-
sponding Fault.

How to Find Your Gentleman Personality Archetype

Are you looking to find your inner gentleman? Changing the way you dress and behave to match the model of a sophisticated and refined gentleman is an excellent way to increase your romantic appeal to women while also cultivating new kinds of friendships that would otherwise not be possible if you behaved in more crude fashions.

For men who are keen to take the dating world by storm, the desire to live up to the title of "gentleman" is a compelling one. Since at least the Middle Ages the gentleman archetype has represented ideal masculine behavior within society. Yet there are many subcategories of ideas behind what kinds of a gentleman can exist. While all gentleman archetypes have common characteristics and traits, some certain accentuate qualities more than others do.
Cary Grant, Sidney Poitier, Ralph Lauren, Sean Connery, Paul Newman, Gregory Peck, Fred Astaire, George Clooney, Will Smith, Leonardo DiCaprio, Hugh Jackman and Antonio Banderas; all of these actors have depicted different archetype of gentlemen in popular movies that influence men in their daily lives. Now it's time to find your inner gentleman, based on one of the common archetypes that define different classes of gentleman from fiction and history.

Gentleman Archetypes and Personalities

The Origins of Gentlemanly Behavior

The concept of gentlemanly behavior comes directly from the courtly ideals of chivalrous conduct exemplified by Medieval knights: Because knights were known for riding horses into battle the word "chivalrous" is derived from the Latin word for "horseman." As the social class of knight developed codes of behavior for how a knight treated servants, his wife, his liege lord and even his enemies developed in an effort to develop stability within the European medieval society, understanding that the manner in which a warrior treated his family, friends and even his employees greatly impacted the stability of nations. While our world has greatly changed and noble classes no longer rule over everyone, the idea that chivalrous behavior practiced by men toward others creates a better, more stable world is as true today as it was back then.

In the spirit of this age-old understanding of courtly and chivalrous behavior, a man who is labeled by others as a gentleman is known primarily by his conduct: Whether he is burning the midnight oil while familiarizing himself with the latest scientific theories or striking up conversations at a high-society party, a gentleman always values honesty, respect for others, respect for knowledge, and a love of good manners. Behavior that brings about feelings of unnecessary offense in others and causes needless conflicts has always been anathema to behaving like a real gentleman; poor form distracts people from successful endeavors by creating drama.

But defining exactly what constitutes a gentlemanly personality is a tricky proposition. Indeed, there are various "types" of gentlemanly conduct. Individuals who are keen to frame their personalities in the mold of an archetypical gentleman may benefit from examining how exactly gentlemen are portrayed in our culture throughout history. Here are just a few great archetypes that may match your personality and give you the perfect model to emulate in your dating life.

1. The Gentleman Socialite

As you might expect the type of person who exemplifies the Gentleman Socialite personality type will positively relish social interaction. This type of person will likely be in their element at a cocktail party where tuxedos are required. They may also hold an outlook on life that would put them more at home in the jazz age of the 1920s than in the present.

Undoubtedly, one of the foremost examples of the Gentleman Socialite personality type lies in author F. Scott Fitzgerald's portrayal of the upper-class man-about-town Jay Gatsby. While Gatsby loves the aristocracy's glitz and glamor, he also shows that it is not necessary to be born into the nobility to exemplify an ideal type of gentlemanly behavior.

In fact, in Fitzgerald's novel "The Great Gatsby," Gatsby is portrayed as having a background characterized by very humble origins. Himself the grandson of poor Irish immigrants, Fitzgerald was no fan of the idea that the circumstances of a person's birth should prevent them from attaining success or social mobility in life.

Despite his modest background the Gatsby of Fitzgerald's novel works his way up the military ladder to become an officer during World War I. He later attends Oxford University on a scholarship and acquires a personal fortune worth many millions of dollars through hard work as a bootlegger.

But most importantly Gatsby shows us that a gentleman is a person who conducts himself with an attitude of fairness and a fierce love of equality. This makes him not only well liked and respected by his peers but a perfect host; someone who can bring people together and create networking opportunities leading to successful endeavors for all involved. Being this type of gentleman requires good manners and a meritocratic outlook, it is true, but behavior in the mold of Jay Gatsby should appeal to people who value standing on their own ground and being their own man. As you might imagine, women find this personality type very attractive.

2. The Gentleman Entrepreneur Personality Archetype

There are no two ways about it: Our culture loves a good story involving entrepreneurs. But entrepreneurship didn't originate with Steve Jobs or Bill Gates; check out Hugh

Jackman's elegant portrayal of P.T. Barnum in the film 2017 *"The Greatest Showman"* for an example of how Gentlemen Entrepreneurs have been around a long time, as well as an example for how they should conduct themselves.

In the film Barnum is portrayed as an optimistic businessman defined by his enormous ambition to succeed despite his humble beginnings, and he cultivates the mannerisms of the upper elite to build himself up into a success. Similarly, when a woman is on a date with a Gentleman Entrepreneur she gets a sense that a relationship with him is likely headed for big things. That is a very attractive quality in a man.

The scenes where Barnum pitches others on why they should join his ventures demonstrate the kind of charm necessary for a gentleman to successfully win others over to support his causes. Sometimes you just have to do the song and dance show to get others to see things from your point of view and how there is value for themselves in working with you.

For another example of a Gentleman Entrepreneur, we should look no further than the 2006 Will Smith film *"The Pursuit of Happyness."* Here, Smith portrays the true-life story of Chris Gardner. Gardner dealt with many struggles in life and was even homeless for a time. As a single father, however, Gardner knew that he wanted to provide a better future for his son. His excellent conduct, excellent manners, and unbeatable ambition make Gardner a real-life example of how gentlemanly entrepreneurial behavior can improve our lives for the better. What woman could resist a man who embodies such qualities?

3. The Gentleman Thief Personality Archetype

In today's world being a Gentleman Thief isn't really about being an actual thief: Like the great fictional character Arsène Lupin, people who live up to the Gentleman Thief archetype are simply very charming, very clever, and very committed to upholding social justice by unorthodox methods within the confines of their own chivalrous code of ethics.

Moreover, people who live up to the Gentleman Thief archetype are adept at problem-solving and love nothing more than a good challenge. And while you're more likely to find today's version of the Gentleman Thief cracking a computer server than a safe, the Gentleman Thief archetype still enjoys the fun of figuring out how things work. He may exploit the weaknesses of systems in order to find opportunities to create the changes he wishes to achieve.

This personality type is charming to the opposite sex because they're always fun to be around. Their love of challenging activities also makes them a great company on dates. But it's the Gentleman Thief's personal charm and good manners that make him a real winner in the dating world: After all, what woman can resist a man with roguish good looks who is as clever as he is polite?

4. The Gentleman Detective Personality Archetype

Despite their good manners and love of fair play a person who exemplifies the Gentleman Detective archetype may have an approach to life that often puts them at odds with society. But what this person lacks in social graces is often made up for by his intellectual brilliance.

Without question the preeminent example of the Gentleman Detective archetype is Sherlock Holmes. Whether you like your Holmes straight out of Arthur Conan Doyle's novels and stories or prefer Benedict Cumberbatch's unique portrayal of the genius detective at work, there are many consistencies to Holmes's personality that anyone of this type should seek to emulate.

Firstly, Sherlock Holmes shows us that being a gentleman isn't necessarily about being wealthy. At the beginning of the Holmes canon, the detective lives on such a modest income that he requires a roommate to help cover his rent at 221B Baker Street; This is how Holmes first meets Dr. Watson.

Secondly, Holmes shows us that we don't have to be social butterflies to conduct ourselves as gentlemen. At times Holmes can be overly-blunt and to the point about trivial matters in life. (Cumberbatch even plays Holmes as a "high-functioning sociopath"). But Holmes always treats people with respect and consideration; there can be no question that he has the best interests of other people at heart.

Thirdly, Holmes demonstrates the fact that real gentlemen should always value learning. Holmes is always challenging himself in unique ways: He cultivates expertise in scientific fields such as chemistry in his spare time. He also regularly practices the violin. The achievements Holmes accomplishes during his stories are due to his application of his vast wealth of encyclopedic knowledge he has accumulated as an autodidact; a self-taught man. Sherlock Holmes is the very definition of what a self-made man can achieve by accentuating his intellectual gifts and applying the lessons of his education to his life.

5. The Gentleman Scholar Personality Archetype

Like the Gentleman Detective, the Gentleman Scholar personality type will have an almost reverential outlook toward intellectual pursuits. But this type of person will also prize imaginative thinking. They will often enjoy creating fantasy landscapes and characters in their spare time, intended to inspire others and pass on valuable life lessons to future generations. Individuals such as J. R. R. Tolkien and C. S. Lewis are perhaps the best examples of this type of gentleman.

Tolkien and Lewis are now regarded as the preeminent fantasy authors of the mid-20th Century. But the two shared more than a love of creating fantastical worlds: Both men were professors of literature at Oxford University; famously, they met with a group of other Oxford writers in an informal fiction workshop/club known as the Inklings. Tolkien and Lewis both valued their small community of fantasy literature aficionados and encouraged one another to take bold steps forward within the fantasy genre.

So, what can Gentleman Scholars learn from the example set by Tolkien and Lewis? Firstly, a true gentleman should cultivate a love of learning for its own sake. Tolkien loved linguistics so much that he created his own languages; Lewis had an enormous impact on English literature study at Oxford and pursued a second career as a public educator and lecturer.

But the two men also shared a deep concern about morality and the well-being of other people. In both their personal lives and in their careers as teachers and authors, Tolkien and Lewis fought fiercely for their fellow human beings' rights.

For these two figures, being a gentleman wasn't just about having good manners. It also meant sticking up for chivalrous behavior precepts and constantly seeking out the right way to conduct oneself in society. If you see something of the Gentleman Scholar in your own values and approach to life, these are great qualities to emulate.

6. The Gentleman Spy Personality Archetype

While the Gentleman Spy won't necessarily be involved in espionage in this day and age, he will probably have a serious interest in politics and the goings-on of the world around him. He may also indulge in a profound love of high living.

Gentlemen Spies always think about the bigger picture; even if their excellent manners make them charming to others, they aren't always satisfied with being just another part of the crowd. They tend to think independently and love being self-starters.

The perfect model of the Gentleman Spy archetype is undoubtedly James Bond. Bond is clever without showing off his intellectual accomplishments; he is brave without harping on his sense of courage; he is dutiful without making a big deal of his undying loyalty to his country. But perhaps Bond's most recognizable attribute is his love of life.

Indeed, a person who lives up to the Gentleman Spy archetype will probably wear their joy of good living proudly on their sleeve. Understandably, people who exemplify this personality type are popular in the dating world: Women find them fascinating because dates are always exciting; their ambitious nature and seriousness also make them compelling mates.

7. The Gentleman Adventurer Personality Archetype

While many of the archetypes are men who are known to have adventures, the Gentleman Adventurer is known for expressly spending his life participating in one adventure or another. Unable to sit still and retire, the Gentleman Adventurer must live every day to the fullest and see everything the world has to offer him.

One of the best real-life examples of the Gentleman Adventurer is Theodore Roosevelt. Had his illustrious ancestors had their way Theodore Roosevelt would have lived out his days in comfort and relaxation as the head of one of New York's most aristocratic families. As the heir to a sizable fortune Roosevelt was expected to live out his life within the cozy environs of Manhattan's upper-class culture. But

Roosevelt had no intention of living an easy or comfortable life.

In contrast to his background the future American President had a zest for adventure that was almost beyond belief. Despite his small size and a weak physical constitution that left him prone to bouts of serious illness as a child, Roosevelt built himself up into a keen outdoorsman and sports enthusiast.

In addition to serving as a soldier during the Spanish-American War, Roosevelt sought out opportunities for big-game hunting throughout his life; he was also a keen boxer during his student days at Harvard College. In fact, one particularly fierce boxing match left Roosevelt partly blind in one eye.

Like Roosevelt, men who exemplify the Gentleman Adventurer archetype love challenges. Although they may be eloquent, the best qualities of Gentlemen Adventurers will be revealed in their actions. They may not talk up their good qualities, but Gentlemen Adventurers will definitely make their mark through their positive life choices.

8. The Southern Gentleman Personality Archetype

In historical terms the Southern Gentleman archetype has always been a part of American culture. Perhaps best exemplified by the writings of author Mark Twain, this archetype is defined by a relaxed approach to the world, a quick and bit-ing wit, and a stylish dress-sense. Like Twain, men who exemplify the Southern Gentleman personality type will also be intellectually sharp without being a show-off.

In the summer, you'll probably find the Southern Gentleman having a drink on their porch while watching the world go by. Their love of order, punctuality, and good manners will always make them pleasant company on a date. While their strict code of chivalry may put them at odds with contemporary culture at times, the Southern Gentleman will always be polite without being condescending. They will always treat everyone they meet with respect.

As you might expect, living up to the Southern Gentleman archetype's values can seem like a tricky proposition. A Southern Gentleman will always hold himself and his conduct to very high standards. But for old-world charm and ease of living, it is challenging to beat this personality type in the dating world. As many women will tell you, no one exemplifies good manners and etiquette quite like a Southern Gentleman. These qualities also make the Southern Gentleman irresistible to the opposite sex.

9. The Quintessential British Gentleman Personality Archetype

If you've ever seen the hit series *"Downton Abbey"*, you're already acquainted with the Quintessential British Gentleman archetype. Throughout the show's six seasons, Robert Crawley, Earl of Grantham exemplifies good British manners and an egalitarian attitude. Despite his high social standing, Crawley is modest and loyal to the people around him. He does not abuse his position of power, and he is quick to resolve any disputes that occur around him.

Men who exemplify this personality type tend to have old-fashioned sensibilities. They value good conduct and are faultless in their social behavior. They may view the world in absolute terms at times, but Quintessential British Gentlemen are always concerned about the justice of their actions. They understand that decisions have consequences, and that the cultivation of thoughtfulness is a must for a real gentleman.

10. The Gentleman's Gentleman Personality Archetype

Of course, even the Earl of Grantham needs supportive allies in life. Like the trusty valet John Bates from "*Downtown Abbey*," the person who embodies the Gentleman's Gentleman archetype is always there to help out people in need and in return, others are there to help them out when they need it, too.

This Gentleman personality type is rarely very flashy, preferring to work behind the scenes to assist others. Yet they often play a leading role in solving major problems. Just don't let their modesty fool you; Gentlemen's Gentlemen live up to a code of honor that they take extremely seriously.

They may not occupy the limelight or seek external validation for their actions, but Gentlemen's Gentlemen set a great example to the people around them. If we're honest with ourselves, they're also the people that we turn to most when the chips are down. Who could want more in a dating partner?

Summary

So, which Gentleman Archetype do you think best fits your concept of the kind of man you'd like to be known as? In truth all gentlemen have qualities of these archetypes within themselves, and a man can be labeled as multiple kinds of archetypes if his personality is complex. Yet listing them out here and reviewing them can assist a man in deciding what archetype he'd be best suited to model himself after. I hope you find this article useful for that purpose.

The Rules of Gentlemanly Etiquette

George Washington is often regarded as the model of the American gentleman. He was widely respected even before he became appointed to serve as the first General of the Colonial Army during the American Revolutionary War and later, the first elected President of the United States of America.

George Washington did not receive a formal education at a boarding school. Instead, he primarily taught himself. His father died when he was eleven years old before he could be sent to boarding school, and he was left to self-educate himself through reading books. While a teenager still, George Washington wrote down a list of rules that he titled, *Rules of Civility & Decent Behavior In Company and Conversation.* The list comes from a French etiquette book *"Bienséance de la conversation entre les hommes'* that was first published in 1595; it is assumed he copied the list from one of the English translations of the book that he came across. The purpose of the list was to guide young men in how to walk the fine line between self-abasement and humility in social atmospheres, and learn self-control. Without these rules there is no doubt that Washington would never have been able to craft a public persona that allowed him to win respect from friends and enemies alike, which made him an excellent leader.

The following list of rules are very similar to what George Washington first wrote down. They have only been slightly adjusted to conform to be relevant to the kind of cultural world we live in today.

1. Treat everyone with respect.
2. Be especially respectful of your elders and others who are your betters.
3. Acknowledge the existence of others. Do not pretend to ignore them.
4. Be considerate of others. Do not embarrass others. Avoid open conflict whenever possible, as this is not a weakness.
5. In the presence of others do not engage in distracting habits like singing to yourself or playing with items that are not your possessions, merely because you are bored.
6. Listen when others speak.
7. Do not sit when others stand.
8. Speak not when you should hold your peace.
9. If you cough, sneeze, sigh or yawn, do it quietly; put your hand before your face and turn aside from others.
10. When eating do not take so large a bite that you must chew with your mouth open; but if others do, refrain from berating them as it is uncivil.
11. Do not hold conversations when your mouth is full. If others do so, listen attentively but do not emulate the behavior.

12. Do not clean your mouth with a fork, knife or table napkin; but if others do so, do not berate them.
13. Drink not too leisurely or too hasty. After drinking you should wipe your lips quietly.
14. When eating in the company of others do not take longer to finish than they do; if you finish before others, wait patiently for them to finish their meal.
15. When attending a feast or party where food is readily available, let the youngest and eldest be fed first. Do not take more food upon your tray than you can rightfully eat, for it is wasteful.
16. Be not angry when eating in the company of others no matter what happens. If you have reason to be angry, show it not.
17. Do not sit yourself at the head of the table, unless you are the master of the house or are given the honor.
18. Be direct in your communications but do not speak louder than necessary.
19. Avoid speaking too closely to other people, to avoid having your spittle fall on them.
20. Do not speak to others while your back is turned to them.
21. Keep your nails clean and short, and your teeth brushed. Bathe daily.
22. Respect the privacy of others; do not read their letters without permission.
23. Do not revel or gloat at the misfortune of another, even if your enemy.

24. When you see a crime punished, you may be inwardly pleased but should show compassion to the plight of the suffering offender.
25. Do not draw unnecessary attention to yourself.
26. Do not compliment others with insincere flattery.
27. Let your discourse in matters of business be short and comprehensive.
28. When visiting the sick or injured do not dispense medical knowledge if you truly lack it. Leave such matters to a physician.
29. In writing or speaking, give each person their due title according to their education and custom.
30. Do not argue with your superior, but instead submit your ideas with humility. A dissenting opinion is not a personal attack on your value as a person.
31. When a person does their best and fails, do not criticize them.
32. When you must give advice or criticism, always consider the timing; such as whether it should be in private or public, and the manner. Above all be gentle.
33. If you are corrected by a superior in public, accept it without argument. If you were wrongly judged, correct it later in private with your superior.
34. Do not make fun of anything important to others.
35. If you are critical of someone else, ensure you are not also guilty of it yourself.
36. Do not hastily believe bad reports about others without any proof of the accusation.
37. Associate with good people. It is better to be alone than with bad company.

38. Always allow reason to govern your actions.
39. Never break the rules in front of your insubordinates.
40. Realize that some things are better kept secret.
41. Do not overly value your own merits and achievements.
42. Do not go where you are unwanted, nor deliver unasked for advice.
43. Do not correct others when it is not your place to do so.
44. What you speak in secret with your friends should remain so.
45. When in the company of others, do not speak in a language they do not understand so as to hide your conversation from others among your company.
46. Do not be quick to talk about things for which you do not have all the facts.
47. Do not be overly curious about the affairs of others which have little to do with you.
48. Do not start what you cannot finish. Keep your promises.
49. Let your recreations be passionate but not sinful.
50. Labor to keep alive in yourself that little spark of celestial fire called your conscience.

Like a young George Washington, it can be useful to copy by hand all the rules of etiquette into your personal journal or diary to help you remember them.

The Book of the Heart

There is a short Japanese document called "*Kokoro no maki*" that was often included in warrior manuals of the samurai. Kokoro means "heart", "center" or "core".

These philosophical musings describe the ideal temperament and disposition for a gentleman. I have included this so that you may read these words to help you re-adjust your frame of mind when you find yourself in troubling times.

When the heart is full of things, the body feels constrained; when it is empty, the body feels expansive.

When there is too much reserve in the heart, love and respect are lost; when it is free of reserve, love and respect are gained.

When the heart is full of base passion, principles are forgotten; when it is free of base passion, principles are remembered.

When the heart is set on gaudy things, appearances are falsified; when it is free of artifice, appearances are real.

When the heart is full of pride, others are begrudged; when it is free of pride, others are respected.

When the heart is full of oneself, others are doubted; when it is selfless, others are trusted.

When the heart is full of error, others appear frightening; when it is free of obstructions, no one is harmed.

When the heart is full of covetousness, others are flattered; when it is free of covetousness, there is no need to flatter.

When the heart is full of anger, words are spoken harshly; when it is free of anger, words are pacific.

When the heart is full of patience, everything can be set in order; when it is not patient, everything collapses.

When the heart is full of self-importance, the goodness of others is ignored; when it is free of self-importance, the goodness of others is appreciated.

When the heart is full of greed, requests are endless; when it is free of greed, nothing extra is required.

When the heart is full of illusion, others are blamed; when it is free of illusion, no one is scorned.

When the heart is full of sincerity, contentment is easy; when it is not sincere, there will be no contentment.

Understanding Good Nutrition and the Cultivation of Your Physique

Admittedly as a young man I did not fully understand the value of good nutrition; I had no good advice in this regard. I ate well at my grandparent's home, but my father and mother had poor diets. During my teenage years I primarily ate frozen bowls of white rice with small amounts of chicken; this diet was unsuitable for packing on sizable muscle mass which squandered the efforts I made in weightlifting. Had I eaten a more suitable protein rich diet I would have built a more muscular body in my teens that would have greatly benefited me before I became a soldier. It is not that I was weak as a soldier but rather I would have been even stronger than I was, had I spent those years from thirteen to seventeen eating a proper diet for gaining huge muscle mass. Sadly, I did not gain as much muscle as I could have because I did not eat enough protein and none of my parents knew this was necessary, since they did not practice a healthy lifestyle themselves.

It is also worth mentioning that developing your physique is necessary for producing healthy children, as an unathletic life could lead to genes related to athleticism becoming recessive and not passed on usefully to your children and descendants, if the body decides they are not relevant for survival and daily life anymore. Exercising your whole life and developing your physique to its potential will prevent this regression while also creating the opportunity for beneficial mutations.

It is the duty of men in the human species to inherit the genes of their ancestors, to cultivate new beneficial gene mutations through a strenuous life of achievement and to pass these beneficial mutations to their offspring. Failing to strive to do this wastes the opportunity your ancestors have bestowed upon you to advance the species further.

Weightlifting should begin when puberty begins, and before these calisthenics should be learned during ages six to eleven. In terms of the path for learning martial arts, a young boy will instinctively start to play wrestling in their toddler years and wrestling should continue to be practiced amongst boys and play fighting with the father until at least the age of seven, at which actual martial art training should begin. Swimming should also be learned around age four or five and practiced regularly throughout childhood, so the child does not accidentally drown themselves later in life.

You must resist the temptation to use steroids, SARMs and other performance enhancing drugs that have side effects that will reduce your lifespan. It will serve your descendants no good if you grow a hugely muscular body but render yourself infertile in the process, or if you die of a heart attack in your 30s or 40s while they are still young children, as you will leave them in a chaotic environment with no proper fatherly guidance.

We should also briefly discuss the topic of sanitation. You want to ensure that you bathe regularly, that you wash your hands with soap and that you keep your teeth clean. These things are all necessary for a good physique, as no one wishes to admire a boy or man who smells terribly and has stained teeth and awful breath. Likewise, it is necessary to wash your hands so that you do not spread diseases into your eyes or mouth by tainting your food or rubbing your eyes after you have dirtied your hands. You must also endeavor to keep your nails clean as well. You only have one body and you must take care of it so that it lasts all your life.

Be in the habit of keeping your shoulders back and walk purposefully everywhere that you go. Do not stare at the ground as you walk unless you are traversing an area that poses risk of stepping on something that could injure or make you slip, such as a rocky area. At all other times keep your head up and avoid looking at the ground when you walk. Be aware of your surroundings.

On that note you should avoid accepting a label of being diagnosed as possessing ADHD. This diagnosis is unfortunately now a weaponized label used against children who exhibit curiosity and rebellion, and instead of parents and teachers educating young boys in how to channel their ambitions constructively, the parents seek to drug the children with sedatives designed to force obedience and compliance. Young boys are naturally supposed to be wandering the landscape with their fathers, learning the rites of passage

necessary for manhood. The factory school system is an artificial construction and as such an unnatural environment for
many young boys. It is no surprise that a boy whose ancestral instincts are to run and play and explore the world, even
learning to hunt and stalk prey with his father, may struggle
if forced to sit at a desk and listen to dull lectures about
mathematics. The lessons must be suffered but a boy's natural resistance against it does not mean anything is actually
wrong with the child at all. In the vast majority of cases, he
merely requires patience and motivation. Drugging him into
compliance will limit his potential in life, in addition to
greatly damaging his health for all his life by refusing him
the opportunity to learn self-control.

Advice for How to be a Natural Bodybuilder

It is very difficult to find reliable information on how to be a
natural body builder as a man. The usage of steroids, even in
the form of TRT (testosterone replacement therapy), has
made steroids very accessible to even young teenage boys.
Most Instagram and YouTube fitness models and channels
are ran by people who are 'enhanced' by usage of steroids
and other compounds, which can make it challenging to find
information that is actually applicable to the majority of men
who are seeking information about how to get into body
building without the enhancement of steroids. The lack of
information can even make people assume incorrectly you
cannot develop a good bodybuilder physique naturally.

The hardest thing is finding good nutrition and training advice. Some of the workouts and training methods of seasoned body builders simply will not work for those who are not likewise enhanced, since using TRT is guaranteed to make you gain muscle mass size even if you do not work out and even if you don't rest adequately, since your body is getting boosts that would otherwise be impossible. While some body builders claim the work they do in the gym is what creates their success, scientific studies on the topic have proven men taking TRT and doing no weight lifting activities will gain muscle mass, and TRT combined with weight lifting results in 4x faster muscle size gains compared to not supplementing testosterone. This is because testosterone supplementation puts your body into a constant state of muscle protein synthesis, which is a state where your body breaks down proteins to build muscle tissue. By staying in an anabolic state far longer than is naturally possible, enhanced athletes gain muscle size and strength at a faster rate than natural athletes can.

This section has been written to gather good information of use and value to men seeking to be a natural body builder, to make the process easier and less confusing.

Why Should You Be a Natural Bodybuilder?

It can seem more beneficial to abuse steroids such as TRT to make quick gains, as the objective of bodybuilding is to develop a great looking physique. Using steroids will allow your body to grow muscle tissue at a faster rate than is possible naturally. This, however, has serious drawbacks. Abusing steroids in this way causes long-term negative health side effects. This is primarily because when you use steroids your body does not only grow muscle tissue in the areas you want it to for a good-looking physique; it also causes growth of other organs and tissues at the same time, and some of this growth is very harmful to you. This is why steroid abusing body builders frequently suffer from heart enlargements, which leads to a significantly high risk of cardiac arrest. There are a wide other range of health problems that anabolic steroid abuse also cause as well, which even includes hypogonadism, testicular atrophy and impaired spermatogenesis (i.e. becoming sterile), baldness, acne, gynaecomastia (ie. growing man boobs), and psychiatric disturbance.

These problems are a consequence of steroid abusing athletes dumping synthetic testosterone and other synthetic growth hormones into the human body. While these synthetic chemicals do trigger an anabolic state and keeps the body in a muscle protein synthesis state for a much longer period than is achievable naturally, the body reacts to this flood of testosterone and growth hormones by ceasing its own natural production. The problem with this is that when your body produces testosterone it also produces a variety of other things, and so when your body stops producing testosterone it also stops producing these other things; one of these things is sperm. Basically, TRT will make you sterile and the longer you are on it, the less reversible your sperm production impairment is.

If you don't want to end up like these young guys who abuse steroids and end up with no sex drives and becoming sterile at a young age, you want to avoid abusing steroids.

With that in mind it is best to remain a natural body builder for longevity, instead of trying to take the quick and easy path. The problem is that so much information has been published on the internet by enhanced body builders who are using steroid cycles, and with steroids even a bad workout and diet plan can still produce gains since the steroids allow the body to enter an unnatural state that is unachievable by non-steroid using weightlifters.

How Long Does It Take to Get a Body Builder Physique as a Natural Bodybuilder?

The length of time it takes to get a classic bodybuilder physique is going to depend largely on your age, as age has the largest impact on how much testosterone and other growth hormones your body can naturally produce. Your own genetics also play a role too, which is why there is a variable; some men have better genes for releasing more testosterone and growth hormones, or genes that better utilize proteins for muscle protein synthesis and tissue repair.

In general, for the average man to gain a classic bodybuilder physique naturally will take 3 to 6 years. However, you should see significant muscle growth and definition in as short as 8 months so long as you are giving yourself proper rest periods, eating good nutrition and working out with proper training intensity. You will generally see a noticeable increase in muscle mass size every 2 to 3 months of consistent lifting, eating and sleeping.

I think it is important to clarify what is meant by a 'classic bodybuilder physique' to manage expectations. Modern bodybuilders who compete in 'classic physique' category are referring to the body type of Arnold Schwarzenegger, who used steroids to achieve that physique.

By 'classic bodybuilder physique' what I actually mean is the kind of physique which is achievable naturally by strongmen of the 19th century, such as Eugene Sandow, who developed their bodies before the existence of synthetic testosterone.

Photo of Eugene Sandow, circa 1893

This physique is achievable naturally by almost any man with 3 to 6 years of consistent training and good nutrition. Developing this physique as a natural body builder will give you lifelong health and happiness with none of the side effects of steroid abuse and you will be able to maintain your gains on a normal diet and lifestyle, which enhanced athletes cannot do when they stop taking the steroids.

Primary Principles Necessary for Building Muscle as a Natural Body Builder

In order to build muscle mass as a natural body building you need to follow three primary principles to be at work in your life,

1. Proper Training Intensity
2. Proper Nutrition
3. Proper Rest Periods Between Workouts

Without these three principles you will not put on muscle mass size.

Let's dive into each of these principles and explain them in detail.

Proper Training Intensity

Your workouts must be designed to maximize time under tension (TUT) or you will not see an increase in muscle size gain. This means that the time your muscles are held under strain (tension) during a lift is the most important factor for weightlifting. Of course, while holding a muscle in a contracted static movement can create tension, holding a position statically only works certain muscle fibers of any muscle group. So you cannot just hold your arms straight in front of you with a bicep bar for several minutes and expect to see huge gains; you need to do full range of motion for the muscle to work all of the fibers in that muscle group, so all of these fibers get to experience a state of high tension sufficiently to exhaust them.

To experience the most hypertrophy with the least amount of time in the gym, you want to focus on compound movements such as the bench press, the military press, the squat and the dead lift to work multiple muscle groups at the same time, and then follow up with some isolation exercises such as bicep curls, triceps extensions, leg extensions and so on, ensuring that you work out the most amount of fibers and have a high amount of time under tension (TUT) for each muscle group you are working out.

Having said this, there is a point where too much volume will put your body into a catabolic state, where it breaks down muscle tissue to use as energy — which is not what you want it to do. While your body will naturally transition between anabolic and catabolic states every day, the catabolic state should be avoided during a weightlifting workout if you want to see significant muscle size gains, especially as a natural body lifter not using steroids to force your body into a prolonged anabolic state.

As a natural weight lifter you should only do a weight lifting workout once a day, of around 4 to 9 sets per exercise with reps performed to muscle failure for each set.

Many enhanced body builders do sets of only 3 or 4, but as a natural body builder you have to push your muscles a little harder to trigger muscle protein synthesis, so it can be ideal to do up to 9 sets per exercise. However, you should avoid using a very heavy lift for these sets, sometimes called an 'ego lift' or a 'max rep' where you try to lift as much as you possibly can. Your ideal rep range should be around 12 reps with the weight. If you make your rep range less than 12 reps (such as if you go to 6 reps to reach muscle failure), you are lifting too heavy for the joints of your body and you will increase your risk of developing training injuries, particularly in the wrists, elbows and knees. You should always avoid doing 'ego lifts' or training like a powerlifter or CrossFit athlete if you want to reduce the chance of injury. It's just not necessary to do that kind of one rep max lifting to put on muscle; in fact, it reduces the amount of time under tension, which means you'll see less size gains working out in such a way.

Proper weightlifting training to develop a body-builder's physique is not about maxing out your lifts; it's about working muscles to exhaustion through several reps and sets, to work all the fibers out in a muscle group so your body can repair them. Damaging your ligaments and joints won't help you develop a physique. Always work the muscles, not the joints. The sweet spot for repetitions each set is reaching muscle failure by 12 reps; this ensures the muscles are being challenged enough to trigger growth, and also helps ensure you are not over-straining your joints and ligaments with too much weight.

On the subject of catabolic states, one thing you should know is that high intensity cardio exercise, such as running, will cause your body to enter a catabolic state. You should incorporate some cardio into your fitness program of course, but know that you should limit daily cardio to 30 minutes to an hour. If you do more cardio than this, your body may not put on as much muscle as it could because it started breaking down muscle tissue to use as fuel for your run. You should also not do cardio on an empty stomach for this reason as well.

Proper Nutrition

Proper nutrition in your diet for natural body building means seven important things,

1. *A Daily Calorie Surplus:* You must eat more calories than your body needs for functioning during the day. Without a surplus your body will instead break down muscle tissue to use for energy, instead of using calories to add more tissue. Generally, you need 250 to 500 calories above your normal healthy calorie intake, as determined by daily calorie intake calculators. This will vary based on your age, gender, height and current body weight so use a calculator to find out what your calorie intake should be, then add an additional 250 to 500 calories to it (ideally, in the form of protein sources).

2. *Lean Protein:* Most of your extra calories should come in the form of protein. Ideally you want protein from meat such as chicken, fish and beef. Protein supplementation from whey protein (which is made from dairy) can also work, although this isn't necessary if you have access to fresh meat. In order to pack on muscle size, your body requires around 0.8 to 1.2 grams of protein per pound of current body weight. So, if you weigh 150 lbs then you need to eat 120 to 180 grams of protein per day, or you will not see an increase in muscle mass size. While some internet fitness gurus claim you must consume this protein during a workout, science says you actually only need to consume the protein within 4 to 5 hours after the workout.

3. *Carbohydrates*: Your body needs carbs in order to break down protein into muscle tissue. Without eating sufficient carbs your body will not be able to break protein down and you will not grow muscle size. You need 100 grams of carbs or more per day. Another thing to mention here is that you must never lift weights or work out on an empty stomach without enough carbs in your system, as your body will enter a catabolic state where it breaks down tissue to use as energy. While a catabolic state is necessary to break down body fat and lose weight, your body always wants to break down muscle tissue before it wants to break down fat reserves, and so by placing your body into a catabolic state it will stop growing muscle mass size.

4. *Dietary Fats:* Despite common misconceptions, fats are good for you in proper amounts, especially when living an active lifestyle. Fats are necessary for your body to create testosterone and growth hormones. Because body builders using steroids are getting testosterone and growth hormones unnaturally, they can afford to do low fat, high protein diets while weight-lifting and still see gains, since they do not have to rely on their own body producing these things made from fats. Basically, you need cholesterol in order to produce testosterone, so eating a low-fat diet as a natural body builder will not work. Natural body builders must produce their own testosterone and growth hormones, so you must eat fats so your body can do this. Ideally you want your fats from monounsaturated fat and omega-3 fatty acids, and to avoid trans fats. Your body needs at least 0.35 grams of fat per pound of body weight per day in order to produce sufficient testosterone and other growth hormones.

5. *Dietary Fibers:* Your body also needs around 35 to 40 grams of fiber per day. While humans lack the enzymes to digest dietary fibers, we need fiber to aid in digestion by producing stools that are solid. So eating a protein rich diet without also consuming enough fibers will cause you to become constipated.

6. *Creatine and other Vitamin Supplementation:* Your body needs certain vitamins to function correctly and create an environment for optimal muscle protein synthesis to occur. While you can gain most vitamins

during the regular course of eating, one thing you cannot normally get is creatine monohydrate. Supplementing with powdered creatine monohydrate will increase your recovery time, allowing you to have more intense workouts. This is because creatine is a necessary thing for your body to convert ATP into energy and without a supplement of creatine your body is limited by how much ATP it can convert per day. If you want to work the most amount of muscle fibers, you need to be depleting them of as much ATP as you can so you need a creatine supplement to do this, otherwise you will need a much longer rest period for your body to build up creatine again. Another good thing for supplementation is glutamine, which your body uses to convert nitrogen into muscle cells. You should eat around 5 grams of glutamine per day, too — most people will get their necessary daily intake of glutamine from chicken meat, eggs, dairy and other sources of protein.

7. *Water:* Water is often overlooked when discussing nutrition for body builders but is of critical importance. Your body needs water in order to transport nutrients through your bloodstream, to perform protein muscle synthesis, to produce sweat for maintaining your body's temperature and to clear toxins from your organs and muscles. You therefore need to be drinking a lot of water throughout the day. If you take creatine supplements, you need even more water since creatine causes water retention. Ideally you should avoid drinking sugary caffeinated

soft drinks as a natural body builder and only drink water; this will not only prevent you from eating bad calories but will ensure you are drinking sufficient water throughout the day so your body can make the most of things to increase your muscle size. Remember, sugar increase insulin levels and too high of insulin levels reduces the release of growth hormones. So, you must avoid bad sources of sugar, such as from sugary soft drinks, as much as possible.

For creatine monohydrate supplementation, I suggest the brand Six Star. This is the brand I use. It can be difficult to find reliable producers of creatine powder as the nutrition industry is largely unregulated in the United States, and this powder is often cut with rice flour — shady manufacturers use too much rice flour and give you far too little creatine monohydrate. Six Star has a good ratio and I find it works very well for me. Six Star also has a whey protein powder as well, which I personally do not use as I get my protein from meat but if your lifestyle makes protein powder better for you then I recommend this brand.

As mentioned briefly in the subject of discussing carbohydrates, you want to avoid working out in a catabolic state while trying to gain muscle mass size. This will cancel your gains as a natural body builder. If you want to lose weight, you should read my article on how to lose weight as a man. This guide shows how to enter a catabolic state for quick fat loss, but doing so will make it very difficult to put on muscle mass size.

What most bodybuilders do is a 'bulking' phase where they focus on providing a surplus of calories to the body for building muscle, which will result in some fat tissue gain. After they have reached their muscle size goals they will do a 'cutting' phase where calorie intake is reduced and they increase the amount of cardio they perform to shed the fat. With enhanced athletes they can workout while 'cutting' and still see some muscle size gain, but as mentioned before it causes long term health problems doing this. As a natural weightlifter you must understand you will gain some fat for a few years while bulking up, which you can later easily lose with cardio and dieting after you gain muscle size. It'll only take a month or two to shed the body fat of your bulking phase; it takes years to gain the muscle mass size of a classic bodybuilder.

Proper Rest Periods Between Workouts

Your body does not build muscle during the actual act of weightlifting itself. When you lift weights you are breaking down the muscles and forcing the body to need to repair them to make them stronger. So what actually builds muscle size is the rest period after a workout.

Specifically, muscle size cannot be put on until after you sleep, because for a natural weightlifter not using steroids your body will not release growth hormones into your blood stream until you enter a sleep phase. It is only during a sleep phase that your body will release a substantial amount of growth hormones. This means that, ideally, after a workout you want to take a nap and trigger this dump of growth hormones so that muscle protein synthesis can begin. However, this is often difficult to do, since having a workout releases adrenaline, which makes you more alert. But don't stress too much about this, because eating a protein rich diet will temporarily increase insulin levels, so sleeping immediately after a meal and workout is not the best thing to do, since your body needs a balanced insulin level to release the most amount of growth hormones during a sleep phase.

As such, generally speaking you should try to sleep at least 3 or 4 hours after you workout and have your post-workout meal in order to maximize your goals. So, if you normally work out in the morning, this may be difficult to do with a normal nine to five job. Yet many men have been able to naturally build great looking physiques without necessarily needing to take a nap after every workout, but this is something you should be aware of in order to maximize your time and energy usage. One thing you can do is workout in the afternoon on your lunch break instead of the early morning, and then eat a protein and carb rich dinner, then go to bed. This will maximize your time usage for those who work a nine to five job.

The ideal scenario obviously is someone who works from home and can control their daily schedule, since you can workout in the morning after a small breakfast, then take a nap by noon and be up to do another workout on a different body part in the evening, triggering another protein muscle synthesis state in your body. Then you can have another protein and carb rich dinner, and go to bed 3 or 4 hours later to trigger yet another release of growth hormones. This allows you to trigger two releases of growth hormones during a single 24-hour period, instead of just one period as you would if you worked a normal nine to five job. Keep in mind, however, that this is only with you working out different muscle groups in a single day; you don't want to overtrain a muscle group by working it out intensely twice a day. As a natural body builder, a muscle group needs somewhere between 24 to 48 hours to fully recover after you have worked the muscles to exhaustion for 4 to 9 sets. If you don't give your muscles time to recuperate, you may cause a major tear in them which could require surgery to repair so don't over-train.

Create a Home Gym for Weightlifting

By now you should have realized that covid-19 has changed the world, especially for those who want to weight lift as a hobby and healthy lifestyle. Even though we are now into 2021, fitness gyms in some states have not re-opened since they closed at the start of 2020. This means you'll need to purchase your own equipment if you want to be able to do natural body building, and it's probably even more important that you have the consistency in your schedule. Owning your own weightlifting equipment and having a home gym in your garage, basement or backyard is therefore critical in order to become a body builder naturally.

With a home gym you can always ensure you work out when you want to, and never need to worry about crowding or state imposed lockdowns on fitness centers. Consistently is necessary to see increases in muscle mass and having a home gym allows you to have this consistency in your training schedule.

Last Pieces of Advice for Developing a Bodybuilding Physique as a Natural Body-builder

Developing a bodybuilding physique as a natural body-builder is a more challenging process than being an 'enhanced' bodybuilder but it will lead to more lasting results. The majority of enhanced bodybuilders cannot maintain their size gains once they come off their steroids, which forces them to continue abusing them and inevitably develop serious health problems. It may be a slower process to make gains naturally but making these gains as a natural body builder will prevent you from experiencing the negative health effects such as enlargement of the hearts, becoming sterile due to low natural testosterone production, and other issues.

The main thing to do as a natural bodybuilder is practice consistency. You must train regularly, eat correctly and get sufficient rest for recovery. You must be committed to this lifestyle to see results.

The goal of the Millennial Gentlemen lifestyle is to encourage men to live healthy lifestyles and make good choices for long term success and happiness. Dying in your

95

fifties from a heart attack because you abused steroids in your 20s and 30s, or becoming sterile so you cannot have children is not a healthy lifestyle. I hope you will follow the advice of this article and make the right decisions in your weightlifting.

Advice for How to Lose Weight In Your Physique When You Become Obese

As a young man you may come to the realization you need to burn off some fat as quickly as possible. It's a common problem in our culture today. We have empty calories in most foods. Even something as seemingly healthy as fruit juice usually has a huge amount of sugar added into it. People tend to put weight on without even realizing it as a result, because they are not active enough to burn off many of the calories in the meals that they eat. And before you know it, you're getting things ready for a great vacation and that's when you notice that you're going to end up bringing a lot of excess fat with you to show off at the beach.

You may realize don't just need to drop the weight; you need to burn fat off as quickly as possible in order to get the most out of an upcoming vacation. And now you're probably wondering how to lose weight fast for men, right?

I know quite a good deal about this topic, as I have struggled with my weight as a man in my own life. Since leaving the military it has been difficult for me to maintain a healthy weight, often because I became so invested into working that I did not keep up a regular fitness regimen.

When you are on a computer from the time you wake up until the time you go to bed, typing hundreds of thousands of words a day then it can be hard to take breaks to go workout. Yet this is the only way that weight loss can be done. Over the past year I have lost fifty pounds of weight while still spending most of my time on my laptop, managing my businesses remotely. So, I think I can provide some useful information for men seeking to lose weight fast.

Through my own research into the topic over the years I have noticed that looking for information on how to lose weight fast for men can be a difficult question for many fitness gurus to answer. People usually talk about their personal weight loss journeys in overly abstract terms. Some people like to fixate on weight loss journeys and considerable changes to their lifestyle. Other people insist that weight loss isn't even possible. But the fact of the matter is that weight loss comes down to a single thing; calorie intake.

If you eat more calories than your body can use then you will put on weight as your body will store those unused calories as fat. And if you force your body to use more calories than you eat in a day then you'll lose weight as this forces your body to tap into those fat stores of energy. Of course, there are a large number of other factors that influence this process but any successful weight loss effort has caloric reduction at the foundation.

The easiest way to lose weight is to practice calorie counting. Calorie counting can be a little difficult at first. But the first step is to simply write down how many calories any given meal is. You should then determine how many calories you're burning per day without exercise. This is known as your basal metabolic rate or BMR. A simple BMR calculator should be able to provide a rough estimate of how many calories you're burning as part of your typical day. Any physical activity should have a caloric number added to it as well. If you walk one mile a day, for example, then you'd add 100 calories to your BMR. This adjusted total is your TDEE or total daily energy expenditure.

Once you have your TDEE it's time to consider calorie cutting. One pound of fat is roughly equivalent to 3,500 calories. You're burning off your TDEE every day. But every bit of food you eat is pushing that total down. When your caloric intake surpasses your TDEE then you'll be gaining weight instead of losing it. Therefore, the best way to lose weight is a calorie cutting strategy that will keep your caloric intake as low as possible.

You'll need to consider how much time you have to lose weight as well. For a man looking to lose weight fast you'll need to do some planning. But in the span of a month most men will be able to drop a significant amount of weight if they are willing to put up with some mild fasting. For a man, how to lose weight fast in a month comes back to that TDEE. Say that a man's TDEE reaches 2000 calories per day. Most meals have a pretty heavy caloric total. A large hamburger is about 700 calories, for example.

One thing that seems to never be explained well in many of the videos and articles that I see online is that you have to use a food scale to weigh your food. Don't just assume that online charts you find for how many calories are in a single meal of chicken breast actually means one single chicken breast; that'd be a huge mistake. For some idiotic reason serving sizes of food is always way smaller than any human would ever consider to be a meal. In my experience a chicken breast you buy at the grocery store is at least three times the size of what the online charts that measure chicken breast calories say a single chicken breast should be. So I highly recommend that you weigh your food before you eat it in order to ensure you stay on track with your dieting.

Now that you understand the basics of counting calories, let me provide you with my best tips on how to lose weight fast.

Stop Putting Calories Into Your Water.

A bottle of soda is around 200 calories. So, the answer to the question of how a man can lose weight fast in a month should be to reduce meal sizes through reduction of calories in each meal he eats. So start drinking plain water without anything added to it, as that just adds more calories to your meal. Yes, this means you must stop drinking coffee, beer and wine.

Consider this: if you usually have three sodas a day then eliminating these sodas from your diet would reduce your calories intake by 600. In less than five days that one simple change would burn off about a pound of fat.

Chances are that one of the reasons you are fat is because you drink many sodas and coffees throughout the day.

Eliminate these drinks from your diet and you will be surprised at how much weight you drop.

This also applies to milk and juices, too. These drinks are advertised as being very healthy for you, and used in moderation they can be, however if your goal is to lose weight you must eliminate calories from your diet and these drinks are high in calorie content compared to how filling they actually are.

Eliminate Your Empty Calories

A man who desires to lose weight fast should begin by considering where some of his empty calories are coming from. These are the calories that don't make him feel full. Drinks are one of the biggest sources of empty calories. As such, you should switch to only drinking water as I mentioned before. For a man how to lose weight fast in a month will next consider the rate of loss.

Candy is one of the biggest sources of empty calories, as candy is rarely ever filling even if it makes you feel good. Donuts, cookies and other kinds of cakes are another kind of empty calories. Basically, anything that is pretty much just sugar is going to be an empty calorie, so cut out the ice cream.

Jog Every Day

I recommend that you jog 30 to 60 minutes a day while wearing a 20 to 50 lb weighted vest, whatever weight you feel you can jog in that is challenging but not impossible. This will maximize the amount of energy you use, causing you to burn calories that would have required you to jog for many more hours of time in order to lose the same amount of weight.

Some people also use treadmills at gyms that can have resistance settings, and that can work as well but wearing a weighted vest places additional strains on your body that require other muscle groups to work hard. Your back, shoulders, neck and abs will get a workout from jogging on pavement with a weighted vest that you will not receive from using a treadmill.

Weigh Yourself Daily

I believe that keeping track of your weight loss is important for staying on track with your dieting. Some people say don't weigh yourself every day, but I need to measure my performance and see what results I get. If I'm not making progress then I know I need to reduce calorie intake and work out more that day. So, I weigh myself every day when I wake up, when I am most dehydrated and after I relieve myself in the bathroom. This is when I am at the lowest weight I will likely be all day other than immediately after an hour long jog.

In addition to tracking my weight loss with my phone app, I also keep track of every pound I lose by keeping a paper log of the day I lost weight and what my new weight was.

I believe it's best to keep the log on the fridge; you're going to be insanely hungry during all of this and posting your log onto your fridge is going to help deter you from eating, as every time you want to open the fridge you're going to have to look at your weight loss log and ask yourself if you want to eat or if you want to lose pounds so you can get the hot babes. The choice should be obvious.

How many calories should you eat to lose weight? The short answer is that you should reduce calories as much as possible. And it's different depending on what foods that you eat. Consider eating apple;. if you can have one apple as a meal, then you'd only take in about 300 to 500 calories a day. That would definitely result in weight loss and I have done an apple fast diet in the past, which did help me lose a lot of weight in a short amount of time.

The larger answer to how many calories should a man eat to lose weight fast comes down to how much he's willing to work at it. If you are willing to only eat three apples a day, and your TDEE is 3,500 then you'd come close to losing a pound a day.

Of course, you probably don't have a TDEE of 3,500. The point is that to lose weight fast you're going to have to force your body into a calorie deprived state where it is forced to live off your fat reserves.

So, the answer to how to lose weight fast as a young man is to try fasting, or at least semi-fasting by reducing your calorie intake to below 1,000 calories a day. I achieve this by eating either one-foot-long Turkey submarine sandwich per day from Subway (with as many veggies as you want, but no dressings or oils) or two bun-less McDoubles from McDonalds.

The next question you might have is, how many days should a man fast to lose weight? People are usually advised not to lose more than 4 lbs per week. But if someone really needs to drop pounds then it's possible to do this. I suggest you start with a one-week trial period to see how this kind of diet works for you. I find it is hardest the first few days but becomes much easier as my body adjusts its hunger levels to the reduced food intake.

In general, this one-week period is a breaking point for most people. A full water only, one sandwich per day intermittent fasting over the course of a week can take a toll on both mind and body.

In the end everything returns to calories. If your body is pushed below its TDEE then it'll burn some fat for energy. And for every 3,500 calories burned you'll lose a pound of fat. Fasting is the fastest means of doing so. But if you only need to lose a smaller amount of weight you can simply determine how many pounds you need to lose and subtract it from a month's worth of caloric intake.

I hope these tips help you in your own weight loss journey.

How to Look Physically Attractive as a Man

How to be attractive to women as a man is a question that is asked by many men, and it's a complicated one because there are many components to it. Many men find this question really hard to answer because it's not really one thing that makes you attractive to women; instead, it takes a combination of things for a man to be very attractive to women. In short, you must project attractive qualities in your appearance and demeanor.

Fortunately for you, I have a great deal of experience dating many women from multiple walks of life. I have dated women of numerous ethnicities, religious backgrounds, income levels, education backgrounds and so forth. Generally speaking, all women who are seeking a man to date and marry are ultimately looking for the same general things in a man. In this essay you will learn how to become more attractive as a man to women.

Men are judged most often on their physical appearance. Whether it's how they're dressed, how they look, or how physically fit they are, women are looking at men and judging them on a physical level. This however does not necessarily mean they only care about your physical attractiveness as a man, but because humans experience the world using their senses and sight is the most important sense for experiencing the world it does mean the visual cues you send women make up a large portion of their toolbox for deciding if a man is attractive.

That said, women don't only identify sexiness in a man based on physical body type; they also use their eyes, ears and other senses to judge a man's mental and emotional states, too. And this plays into how attractive a woman perceives a man to be. People will never fall in love with a person they don't respect. This means cultivating qualities that people in general respect in men.

Understand the Types of Attraction

You should understand that there are three types of attraction:

1. Physical attraction (what you look like)
2. Mental attraction (your personality)
3. Emotional attraction (your capacity to make her feel good)

Understand that attraction is not a choice, it's a feeling. Many women are very primal in their attraction, following their instincts to determine what is attractive in a man. As women are predominantly hypergamous due to evolution, they generally seek out a man to be their romantic partner who appears to be their 'better half'; a man of higher social status than herself. This can be based on income, but it can also be based on projecting strong athletic ability, too, as athletic men are perceived higher in social order.

Developing Your Physical Attraction as a Man

The easiest way to look better physically is to eat well and exercise regularly. If you're a man then you want to avoid excess body fat, which is a sign of a sedentary lifestyle and poor diet.

The best thing a man can do for his appearance is to work out and try to build muscle mass. If a man is over-weight, he should try to focus on losing the fat and then work on gaining muscle mass. After your workouts you also need to get enough sleep so that your body has time to re-cover and repair the damage that was done to your body dur-ing the day. It's also important to eat a balanced diet that is high in protein and good fats and low in carbs and sugars, and to exercise regularly.

Focus on your health by getting plenty of sleep, eat-ing well, and exercising often. Wear clothes that fit well and suit your body type. Wear a cologne or perfume that pleases you.

For more detailed information on developing your physical attraction to women as a man, read our articles about fitness and health for men.

You don't have to spend hours in the gym every day or spend thousands of dollars on plastic surgery to look more attractive. You can also look more physically attractive by simply paying more attention to your grooming and hygiene.

You also need to dress well and appropriately, projecting power in your appearance.

To look more physically attractive as a man, start by wearing clothes that fit, and that aren't too tight. The goal is to look smart, so avoid the tight skinny jeans, and instead wear classic jeans and trousers that fit well. Find a good barber and get a haircut that suits your face shape.

A good haircut is important, but it doesn't matter how good your hair looks if your face doesn't match it. Some men naturally look better with facial hair, but many don't. You must be confident, have a sense of humor, and be able to show that you're a good catch.

Developing Your Mental Attraction as a Man

Developing mental attraction as a man boils down to a few simple things.

1. Be ambitious and hard working.
2. Be a good listener and a good conversationalist.
3. Be a gentleman and treat your date with respect.
4. Be someone she can trust.

Each of these things has the common theme of projecting 'value' to a woman.

- Being ambitious and hard working projects value that you can be a good provider to her and her future children.
- Being excellent at conversation means you project value as a person that she will find mentally stimulating.
- Being a gentleman and treating her with respect projects value as a romantic partner.
- Being someone she can trust projects value that you can be her ally.

The most important thing is to be yourself. Just be yourself. If you're trying to be someone else, it won't work. If you're trying to be a certain way to impress someone, it won't work. You can't do that. You must actually be the person you project for attraction to be developed. So the best thing to do is be confident, be yourself, and be inviting.

The most important thing to remember when you're working to look more physically attractive is that it's not about you being more attractive to yourself; it's about developing qualities that the majority of women find to be attractive. The majority of men look in the mirror and they're worried about how they look to women, because they know they are not in shape. So one of the easiest ways to develop your mental attraction is to also develop your physical attraction; a man who is in shape feels more attractive because he knows that he is. And that powerful feeling of knowing you are something allows you to project confidence which women find to be attractive.

Develop Your Emotional Attraction as a Man

Emotional attraction is one of the most important types of attraction. It's the foundation of a relationship. If a woman doesn't feel a strong emotional connection with you, she's not going to feel comfortable in a relationship with you.

I'm a big believer that attraction is an emotional process, not a logical one. So, when I say that you need to be emotionally attractive, I mean you need to make a woman feel good emotions when she is around you. The way to do that is to project positivity, which requires projecting stoicism during a crisis or emotionally difficult moment. Women expect men to be pillars for them to lean on when things become difficult, and she loses attraction to a man she has to take care of like he was a child.

In order to be more emotionally attractive as a man, you have to show that you are in touch with your feelings. The great thing about emotional attraction is that it's not really something you can teach. It's a skill you have to learn on your own. If you're interested in learning how to be emotionally attractive to women, you should start by being emotionally engaged with your friends, family, and colleagues.

One thing to avoid is being too emotionally vulnerable. Women often say a man who is 'vulnerable' is attractive, but women do not enjoy crybabies and date men who are desperate. Desperation is not an attractive quality. What women actually mean by emotionally vulnerable in a man is one whom they feel understands their emotions and indulges them. Instead of the man being vulnerable, what women want is a man they can vent their own emotions to and be vulnerable with, and because she is connecting with you emotionally while sharing, she feels you are being vulnerable with her (even if it's really just her doing all of the emotional sharing and you are merely listening and comforting her).

The most attractive personality trait for women is emotional stability. The second most attractive trait is kindness. This plays into rejection, because many women will test a man's emotional fortitude by being hard to get to see how he reacts. Because you can't get through life without getting rejected, it's important to know how to not let it bother you, and how to move on; doing so can actually make a woman desire you more and chase you instead.

The first thing to do to build up your emotional attractiveness to a woman is to put yourself out there. Start going to events, join social clubs, and take up hobbies that put you in the public eye. The more people get to know you, the more they'll like you. The more other people like you, the more attractive you become to women. Again, women tend to be hypergamous and they desire men of higher social status, and a marker of social status is the clout and influence you possess among other people. A woman therefore finds a man who is well liked by others as very attractive.

Emotional intelligence is a trait that women find very attractive in a man. By being emotionally intelligent, you can build stronger relationships, experience less conflict, and connect with people more deeply. So having all of these factors in your life is a sign to women that you have emotional intelligence.

110

In the end, be attractive to women by being a man. So, be a man. Don't overthink it.

Advice for Grooming and Haircut Styles

Knowing which haircut best suits your face is important for a man to look sharp, especially when he is wearing a suit. While this subject is not complicated, it does require some basic knowledge about the most common types of faces and hairstyles for men. With this knowledge, haircut ideas for your next appointment at the barber will be straight forward.

If you are a man who feels like a fish out of water when he visits the barbershop or stylist salon, you have come to the right article. By reading our guide will learn to discern if short, long, straight, or curly hair suits you best, as well as if you would look good with or without a beard. We have put together a guide to help you understand your hair from a barber, hairdresser, or stylist perspective. When you are asked the classic barber question, "How do you want me to cut or comb your hair?", some men usually have an idea of the style and cut they would like to have, but some men struggle to communicate it clearly.

Some men also might print out a photo of a hairstyle from a famous male celebrity they'd like to mimic, but what hairstyle looks good on one man might not be as good of an option for yourself. This is because we do not all have the same head shapes and sizes.

In this article we will shed some light for you on this topic, explaining first the different types of faces and the male hairstyles that best go with them. We will then educate you

113

about classic men hairstyles that are timeless and guaranteed to make a man look sharp when he wears a suit.

A gentleman should, whenever possible, visit a barber, not a hair salon. The gentlemen who take up the craft of barber are to be supported with the patronage of gentlemen in their communities, and if you are a male reader of this book then you are now among our ranks. Do your part to support your fellow gentlemen.

Where Should a Man Get His Hair Cut? Barber Vs. Salon Stylist

There can be confusion between what the difference between a barber and a salon stylist is, so let's discuss this at the start of our article. A barber is someone whose occupation specializes specifically in the cutting of men's hair in traditional, short styles, as well as the grooming of male facial hair. By contrast a salon stylist is trained to cut longer, fuller hair styles for both men and women, but mostly women. Between the two of them, barbers tend to use clippers and razors and salon stylist use scissors and supplementary styling techniques. A salon stylist may also be called a hairdresser.

As a man who frequently travels I have had my hair cut in many cities around the United States. My personal experience with going to salon stylists have been mixed. There are some salon stylists I have met who do not know how to cut a proper fade. I've experienced the misfortune of a salon

114

stylist confusing a fade with a high and tight on several occasions, and one time a hair salon stylist actually shaved my head by running an electric razor up the middle of my skull because she thought a fade, as a "military style haircut", was a buzzcut. This forced me to have to cut all of my hair off. I looked like a punk rocker for months while needing to grow my hair back out. I was not thrilled about this as I have a round style face, so such a short cut made me look silly.

Yet this does not mean there are not good salon stylists who can cut short men's haircuts; some of the best fades I ever had were done by a female hair salon stylist. Yet a barber specializes in the cutting of short men's hairstyles and no barber worth their salt will ever screw it up. Consequently, a man is better off going to a barber shop for his haircuts if there is one near him.

Types Of Faces and Men's Hairstyles that Go Best with Them

To learn the type of face and features you have, let's talk about the most common faces and the hairstyles that suit you best:

Triangular Face

Triangular faces stand out for having wide jaws yet narrower foreheads. A man with a triangular face should select a haircut style that will have the effect of softening his jaw area and optically widen his face's upperparts to balance it out.

Men with a triangular face should select a hairstyle that gives the appearance of adding volume to the upper half of the forehead with a cut that is not too long, so hair does not fall below the face, as triangular faces are already bottom heavy.

You may also consider growing a goatee type beard to make the chin appear more prominent (breaking the horizontality of that area) or adding sideburns (that are finite and long), to discount volume in the maxilla area and add length to the oval.

Heart Shaped Face

The best haircut types for those with a heart shaped face (also called an "inverted triangle face) are hairstyles with volume on the forehead and ears. Your goal here is to try to reduce the difference in size between the forehead and the jaw.

The best thing to do is go with male hairstyles that are natural and soft, perhaps betting on a fringe that falls on the forehead, but always with some volume. You should also avoid very short hair at all costs, as deeply short haircuts will exaggerate your chin or expose your features too much.

Elongated Face

Men who have this type of face can take advantage of hairstyles with long hair and look more attractive. Our advice is that men with elongated faces should wear a haircut with more volume on the upper part (both on the forehead and the sides of the head).

Fades and crests are a hairstyle that greatly favors men with this type of face, although you should avoid making the haircut too short on the sides (especially if there is a difference with the rest of your head since you run the risk of giving the impression of prolonging your face).

Growing a beard will also look good on a man with an elongated face, so long as you trim it down so that it works to frame your features. Otherwise, your face will look too long.

Oval Face

Oval faces are considered ideal for a man, as they are both elongated and rounded in equal parts, keeping the proportions of the face very well. Those who have this type of face shape are lucky, as any type of hairstyle will suit them, as will most types of facial hair beards, goatees, mustaches, and so on.

Some general rules still apply for men with oval faces. You should try to avoid wearing hairstyles with many bangs, as this will make an oval face look more elliptical than it really is. The ideal would be to choose a hairstyle to bring the hair up or to the side, clearing the forehead that is very flattering for this physiognomy type. Wearing short hair hairstyles that are shaved on the sides can be an excellent option.

Square Face

The haircut that suits the square face will depend on whether a man wishes to mark or hide his features. For keeping them, the idea is to have a short or very short haircut, but if you like longer hair, you can also take advantage of a haircut style that does not cover the forehead and where the hair falls on the sides.

You should try to use your hair volume to round out your features, so it is therefore a good idea to choose a hairstyle with more hair in the head's central part. This way, you will look good when you wear a suit.

118

Round Face

If you are one of those men who have a round face shape you may be overweight, although some men can have very round faces even if they are no. Round faces will often make a man look much younger and childish if the man has too short of a haircut. The best solution to avoid this is to use hairstyles that are neither too short nor too long (a half-length hair with bangs, for example, would be a good option), as this will help to disguise the roundness.

    The idea is to concentrate the greater volume of your hair in the upper part of the head; playing with the volume or bringing the hair up will create an effect where the rounded features will be more concealed.

Diamond Face

The diamond face shape is considered by many to be the most masculine and ideal face shape for men, although it is also considered rarer than other shapes of male faces.

    As for the types of hairstyles that go well with the diamond face shape, since it is unnecessary to reduce or mask certain areas (because everything is well balanced and portioned in this face shape), you have a lot of freedom to choose.

Classic and Timeless Hairstyles for Men

This section of our guide will show you a list of some classic male hairstyles that make a man look good when he wears a suit. We will show you the most classic hairstyles you can get with short hair, as well as with more modern longer hair.

In general, all the hairstyles that we will show below are very easy to care for and maintain, although long hair has particularities that we will discuss, too.

Fade

The fade hairstyle consists of a men's haircut with a gradient on the sides of the head. The majority of the hair is kept on the upper part of the head, with the sides' hairlines progressively reduced as they descend the head. The fact that the length of the hair is progressively reduced gives it a touch of discretion, but you can give it your personality by deciding the brand of the cut.

The fade haircut is a classic male haircut, and is typically regarded as the primary 'military-style' haircut for men. It is very low maintenance and usually does not require any effort to style, such as with gels.

Side parting

The side parting haircut for men was especially popular from the 1920s to the 1940s, and became popular again during the 1960s. This haircut style has seen a revival of interest over the past decade as a simpler to-accomplish option in contrast to the slick back, another popular classic haircut.

As the hair style's premise is a straight short back and sides, the style is flexible and will suit most hair types and face shapes. All things considered, this can risk exposing a balding spot if the hair is excessively long and meager on top.

The styling gel you should utilize relies upon your hair thickness: those with thicker hair are better suited to using hair styling paste, while a matte clay works best for less thick hair types.

While the haircut looks simple and straightforward to style, parting the hair can be a precarious task. You'll need to identify where your hairs natural parting is at and then comb from that point. To locate the hair's natural parting point, simply comb your hair back and you'll see where the parting begins.

Slickback

The cutting edge slick back first came into popularity during the 1920s. At that point, it was valuable to have a haircut that would look sharp when wearing a cap or a hat (the type of which marked a man's social class up until the mid twentieth century). The Slickback has never gone out of fashion as a popular men's hairstyle.

Straight hair is best for this – the more twist you have, the harder it is to slick back appropriately. Concerning what face shape suits this style, it's entirely flexible, as it will permit facial highlights (like whiskers, mustaches) to be more noticeable, with the hair basically confining the face. Tragically, for those with a retreating hairline, the slick back look won't be ideal as it'll make your balding forehead far more noticeable.

The back and sides should be tightened, with graduation up to the somewhat heavier top. In case you're going for an undercut style, there should be a separation here; however, blending the hair is better if you have a particularly fine hair type.

To style a Slickback haircut, you should blow-dry the hair back. A traditional slick look utilizes a water-based grease and comb the hair over while it is still wet.

Shoulder Length Cut

Exemplary and refined, this long hairstyle for men has become popular for several decades as longer hair styles have come into fashion, likely because it is flexible enough to be adjusted to match different fashion styles. If you'd like to look like Keanu Reaves as John Wick, or Jared Padalecki as Sam Winchester, this is the haircut for you.

Presumably, the hardest piece of accomplishing this style is growing out your hair. You will look especially silly and wild for several months while growing your hair out to the necessary length to be able to accomplish this hairstyle, yet do not let that deter you if this is the style of hair you really want to go for.

Something to keep in mind with longer hair styles is that many hair types often won't behave as you expect they will. Straight hair won't tame as easily as hair that already has a natural wave to it; similarly, men with naturally curly hair will find it challenging to keep their hair from frizzing out into all directions at the top of their head.

Yet with this haircut style you should not rely too heavily on saturating your hair with styling products, as this hairstyle is at its best when it looks natural. So, you could attempt some salt splash to include non-abrasiveness for a messier take. Texturizer can help tame the frizz out of naturally curly hair, and salt spray can soften hair that is too straight.

How to Dress Well

Gentlemen are those men who dress like men should – with a little bit of swagger. What does that mean? It means you dress like a man who can carry his own weight. You don't dress like a girl and you don't dress like a child. This means abandoning the kinds of clothing that are "nerd" branded, like t-shirts of superheroes and cartoon characters, and instead dressing like a traditional adult man.

Classic men know that the way they dress says something about them. If they're wearing a suit with sneakers, they're dressing for the job they want. If they're wearing a suit and loafers, they're dressing for the job they have. These signals about your clothing reveal a great deal about a man in important ways that alter how others interact with you.

When it comes to dressing, a classic man always looks well put together. He knows what looks good on him and always looks like the best dressed man in the room. He's not afraid to experiment with different cuts and styles of shirts, but he knows how to wear them.

The Easiest Way to Dress Like a Classic Gentleman

If you want to dress like a classic man, then you need to have a minimalist approach. The clothes in your wardrobe should be toned down in colour and have simple cuts that fit the body shape you want to project. You'll want to avoid loud patterns and fabrics, as well as anything extra.

There are a few classic pieces of clothing that will always be classic and will never go out of fashion. The first piece of clothing that comes to mind is a suit and tie. If you're not in a work environment, then wearing a suit and tie is a must.

To be a classic gentleman, you need to have a classic style. A classic style is about having a sense of style that's timeless and timeless means you can wear the same outfit every day and it'll still look good. So, when it comes to dressing like a true gentleman, there's nothing more classic than a solid dark grey suit. It's versatile, easy to wear to all occasions, and never goes out of style.

When you're dressing like a classic gentleman, you need to be well put together. Classic gentlemen dress according to their social status. As a beginner, there are a few things you can do to help you get in the mindset of a classic gentleman. You should look for garments that give you a sense of power. This is why wearing a suit, for example, can make you feel like you have the ability to command others as well as project to others that you have this ability. So, you should ensure you are wearing the core elements of classic

126

gentleman style; a proper suit, a nice shirt, a good tie and a pair of shoes. If you are going out you should also have your accessories such as tie clips and shirt cuffs.

If you want to be a classic gentleman, you need to dress like a classic gentleman. It's important to dress well, and it's a good idea to dress to impress. When you're dressed well, you're putting your best foot forward and showing people that you're confident in yourself.

Classic men are not afraid to stand out and be different. They wear what they want to wear and dress the way they want to dress, and they wear it with confidence and pride. They don't let anything, or anyone stop them from being the best versions of themselves.

If you're looking to look like a classic gentleman, you really don't need to be overly fussy or spend lots of money on clothing. The best way to dress like a gentleman is to avoid anything that looks too trendy or trendy at all. You want to make a statement of timelessness and sophistication.

You should also be comfortable in your own skin. Wear what makes you feel good and comfortable and be sure to avoid anything that makes you feel uncomfortable. You'll look better and feel better when you're in a good mood. The best way to ensure you look and feel comfortable is to have your clothing tailor fitted at a local tailor or alteration shop. Don't just wear your suit off the shelf– get it tailored to fit you properly. You've got to be comfortable, cool, and confident when you're in a suit. If you're wearing a suit and you're still sweating and uncomfortable, then you're not looking the best.

A classic man should always be well-groomed and well-dressed. He shouldn't show off too much of his personal style or preferences, but he should look well-groomed and well-dressed. He can be a bit more casual in his dress, but he should always look put together.

There's an old saying that says, *"If you're going to buy something, buy it once and buy it right."* That's true for all of your purchase decisions, not just clothes. Remember that.

How to Find Your Fashion Style as a Man

There are many men out there in the world who feel lost when it comes to fashion. Fortunately, there are loads of resources available for men to help them find their style and the Millennial Gentleman is one such resource. If you're a guy who's always wanted to dress nicer, or even just a guy who wants to learn how to dress better, there are some easy ways you can go about it that are time tested and proven to work. If you're a guy who's interested in fashion, then you need to know how to find your fashion style. You can't be a fashion victim if you want to stand out from the crowd and be viewed as a stylish well-dressed millennial man.

Some men are often hesitant to step out of their comfort zones to explore new fashion style, as they fear doing so may jeopardize their masculinity. This article has been written to focus on proven and timeless fashion advice for men that will never steer you wrong. If anything people may be jealous of how good you look if you adhere to the advice in this article.

How to Dress Stylishly as a Man

Being stylish is all about confidence. If you don't feel confident about your fashion choices, then it's harder to put yourself out there and show the world what you're wearing.

Men often think they need to wear a specific type of clothing that is currently trendy in fashion magazines in order to look good. Instead, you should conform to time proven styles of men's fashion. Regardless of what some fashion bloggers claim, you should NOT wear just whatever you want. Different dress attire is socially acceptable in certain settings and inappropriate in others, and if you go against the grain you are less likely to be perceived by others in the manner that you actually wish to be viewed by others. Your clothing says a great deal about you to others, and one of the most important things it says is how well you can adapt to fitting into a group.

Another factor to consider is that low-quality cheaply manufactured clothing can easily fall apart, sometimes literally at the seams. Clothing that has been produced to ride fashion trends are what is referred to as 'fast fashion', as it has been quickly produced to take advantage of the short window of time these fashion trends are still going viral. The downside to this is that fast fashion manufacturing methods require cutting corners, so the materials and sewing process tend to be low quality. For this reason, I don't recommend trying to follow trends in this way and instead focus on time-less classic men's fashions. This will ensure your clothing is long-lasting, something you could potentially wear for many years.

One thing that is helpful is styling your wardrobe around a certain gentleman personality archetype you wish to convey. This means adopting the look of certain famous fictional and real gentlemen in popular media such as movies, television series and novels, in order to present yourself as possessing the readily identifiable qualities these archetypes convey to onlookers.

When it comes to finding your style as a man, there are a few tips to keep in mind. First off, define your personal style. What does it mean to you? Then pick clothes that suit that style.

Generally speaking, you can't go wrong pairing a white long sleeve shirt with a brown blazer, jeans, and a comfortable pair of shoes. There are more effortless things you can try to spice up your look, such as untucking your shirt and rolling up your sleeves.

This doesn't suggest that you cannot still find ways to express individuality even if your style of dress is con-forming to a standardized dress code. As an example, back in my Army days soldiers typically expressed their individu-alism in uniform by the style of boots they wore and how they handled their boot laces. In those days we still primarily wore a woodland camo uniform with black shined boots, and soldiers could purchase and wear a wide variety of ap-proved black boots ranging from the standard issue grunt boots to paratrooper boots, to jungle boots. As laces on boots must be tucked in per Army regulations, many guys came up with novel ways of tying excess boot lace around the top of their boots before finally tucking the remaining lace in, and this created various pattern designs. This was within regulations and allowed expressions of individuality.

In another example, when I wear a tie I often wear a tie clip. I have a variety of tie clips for numerous types of occasions. Some of my favorite tie clips are novelty clips in the form of swords, as I am a sword enthusiast and historical fencer. I also have some 'nerdy' tie clips in the form of He-Man's Power Sword and the Master Sword from The Legend of Zelda that sometimes I might wear in a more relaxed setting. Wearing this type of tie clip expresses individuality while also conforming to appropriate dress codes. Furthermore, I like wearing French cuff shirts with colorful velvet blazers, notable maroon and blue blazers. I like to wear velvet blazers because they are a classy evening wear which can also be worn casually with slacks or jeans when going out for a night on the town.

You don't have to follow fashion magazines or what everyone else is wearing, but you should ensure your clothing conforms to an established fashion trend that is timeless and classic. This does not necessarily mean you must dress expensively; a classic rugged look such as that worn by the characters Sam and Dean Winchester from the TV series Supernatural meets this criteria. If you are going out to a strip mall steakhouse or a local pub for a first date, or a hike in the woods, dressing this way will be appropriate and generally present yourself well, too. Again, the dress code should depend on the activity and venue you are planning to attend. It would be strange for me to wear a velvet blazer literally everywhere just as it would to wear a tanned leather jacket and logger boots everywhere.

Finally, you should wear an appropriate men's haircut. You don't want to be too extreme or radical in this regard either, and instead select a haircut that will look well with the shape of your head and type of hair that you have.

Advice for Choosing Men's Pants

When choosing a pair of jeans, you're looking for the ones that fit your body shape. Your jeans should form your waist, and they should also be comfortable around your hips and butt. The ends of your pants legs should not drag under on the ground, either. These are the most important aspects of pants. Don't overthink it more than is necessary.

Finding Your Fashion Style as a Gen Z Man

Gen Z or Generation Z is regarded as men born between 1995 to 2015. These are people born in the digital age. Gen Z seems to modernize everything they touch, along with things considered strict and by-the-book such as gender roles, femininity and masculinity, and fashion.

Some Gen Zers are quick to want to tear down traditional rules and rewrite them for the sake of self-expression, but humans are social creatures and it is our ability to utilize easily identified traits and qualities that makes it easiest to cooperate with others, especially when you need to engage with people of many different social class backgrounds and age groups. Therefore, there is still a subconscious expectation for men to dress accordingly and it is good to learn these rules so you can navigate life successfully.

No matter how modernized fashion is now, these style rules apply because fashion is still cyclical. Collared shirts, coats, classic slicked-back hair, and other things that used to be a staple for men decades ago are still capable of making powerful statements about yourself in today's fashion culture world. Following these proven fashion staples will ensure you wear a timeless style that incorporates comfort and convenience.

Hipster fashion style is surprisingly on the rise. We've all lived through the time when flannel shirts, sweaters, scarves, boots, and beanies were everywhere. It was not long until people began to lust for something more exciting. Hipster clothing is getting its redemption now. It is not hard to see why. Almost everyone can rock an artsy, photography enthusiast, Tumblr-inspired style.

Today's hipster fashion is modernized, incorporating the essence of the classic artsy and relaxed aesthetic with trends, thus giving birth to a crisp, comfortable, and effortless style. Colorful coats and patterned shirts are incorporated to spice up the classic sweater topped with a scarf, fitted pants, and boots.

A Millennial Man Should Avoid Adopting an Athleisure Style for All Occasions

Curating one's style takes a lot of time and does require a budget. In an effort to minimize the time spent shopping for clothes and to maximize budget, many millennial men these days prioritize comfort and function as easy bases for all of their wardrobe. This style is most commonly known as "athleisure", which is where people wear things like gym clothing or sportswear as casual everyday wear. While it is tempting to want to wear sweatpants and hoodies everywhere you go as you attend school classes, go to work and even go on dates, the reality is that dressing this way can present you as a person who does not invest any effort into his appearance. On dates it comes across as lazy and can even be interpreted as insulting, especially as women generally do not go on dates dressed in sweatpants and hoodies — you should match the effort of your date because when a girl feels overdressed because you underdressed, she feels embarrassed and insulted.

 You should therefore avoid wearing athleisure attire when you are attending a social event that has nothing to do with athletics or sports; it's fine to wear athleisure to the gym or to go hit up Wal-Mart for some groceries, but you should not wear it to a party, to school classes or on a first date. It is better to dress more appropriately, as the mature adult male you are, and not to dress like you are a child wearing P.E. clothing. This is the reason why athleisure is said to be "lazy." Lazy fashion is wearing anything thrown together that is easy to wear, such as oversized shirts, tank tops, yoga pants, leggings, and sweatpants. It takes little to no effort, even if it might be comfortable.

Athleisure is also very popular among hip hop artists and social media influencers, who claim it makes them look 'urban'. The reality is that they have made themselves walking billboards for Nike, Adidas and Reebok. Even when they have their own branded merch, the reality is they often choose these styles because they are cheap to manufacture and after slapping their own branded logo onto them, can mark the sale prices up 500% or more compared to what it costs to manufacture.

In my personal opinion there is nothing masculine about being a corporate shill who believes clothing mass produced in a sweatshop is fashionable just because it has a multi-million-dollar corporation's brand logo on it. As a young man you need to decide if you want to dress like a drug dealer, or if you want to dress like a gentleman. My advice to you is to dress for the lifestyle you want to have. This has nothing to do with ethnicity; it is entirely about your attitude.

Exploring your unique fashion style as a man is something I heavily encourage men to do today. Fashion choices and the clothes we wear say more about us to others than we would like to admit. Your fashion style represents who you are as a person and conveys certain values. It tells everyone a lot about your personality before you even speak. It also gives people an impression of who you are. Therefore, presenting yourself in a style that you are comfortable with, and you think represents you properly is major.

As a man, your fashion taste is crucial for your expression as a person, because good fashion requires discipline, effort and has principles. Take charge of the image you convey to others about who you are and what values you represent by dressing well as a gentleman.

How to Brush and Shine Dress Shoes and Boots

It was once considered an essential skill for a man to know how to brush, polish and shine his leather dress shoes and boots. Tragically most men today will never learn the craft unless they join the military, one of the last institutions with a dress code that requires a man to brush his shoes and learn to do so. Yet even this long-lasting tradition among soldiers has started to fall out of fashion, as desert style jungle boots have become standard issue by the US Military — these boots cannot be polished. Furthermore, many soldiers now wear glossy faux-leather shoes that do not require polishing.

So perhaps I am among the last generation of men who learned how to shine his shoes and boots in the Army the old-fashioned way. As such it may be my duty to pass on the techniques my drill instructors taught me to future generations of men. Which brings us to this guide on how to brush and shine your dress shoes and boots.

Organizing your Shoe and Boot Polishing Kit

Every man who owns leather shoes and boots must own a kit to take care of them. Leather rots easily when not protected from the elements and the only way to protect them is to polish them with paste. This is the functional purpose of polishing boots and shoes. Leather shoes and boots that are well polished and cleaned regularly will last for many years; shoes and boots that are not cared for properly will rot within days.

To properly polish your shoes requires the proper supplies and tools for the task. While there are many so-called polishing kits sold on the market today, my opinion is that most are poorly created. Kiwi is the market leader in shoe polish and it is the brand most men purchase, as well as their starter kits. However, I do not recommend them. I find their polish to be inferior to other manufacturers and the tools of their kits to be poor for the cost. Kiwi has become the market leader by producing inexpensive paste and tools with a large markup.

You should instead use Lincoln branded shoe polish, which is a softer and more creamy brand of polish that is also water-proof and does not crack after drying like Kiwi typically does.

Additionally, the size of bags and boxes included with many pre-built shoe polish kits are too small for the accessories you need to properly polish your shoes, which with my directions includes a heat gun. Subsequently I use a large clear makeup bag and I suggest you do the same for your kit, too.

The essential items you will need for your shoe polish kit are the following:

- 1 Clear makeup bag, large size
- 1 heat gun(that will fit inside the makeup bag)
- Cans of black and neutral Lincoln shoe polish
- 2 small shoe polish applicator brushes (one for neutral and one for black)
- 1 good shoe medium sized polishing brush made from horsehair.
- 1 dual sided shoe cleaning brush.
- 1 hand towel
- A bag of cotton balls, or alternatively a piece of ripped white t-shirt.
- Several ziplocks bags to put your cans of shoe polish and brushes into separately.

You may also, as an option, wear disposable latex gloves if you are very concerned about getting your hands dirty, and for beginners this could be a good idea. Personally, I don't bother because I don't get my hands very dirty while polishing my shoes.

As my original shoe polish kit is something I assembled over twenty years ago as a young man in the Army, I have assembled a new kit from supplies purchased from Amazon so that I can show you how easy and how affordable it is to put together a good shoe polish kit. You do not need half of the things that are advertised to men for shoe polishing — you don't need gizmos like electric shoe buffers and all of this other nonsense.

On the subject of whether to use brown polish for brown boots and shoes, it depends. If the leather is not true brown but another shade of brown, such as a burnished brown or oxblood or something else, you should use neutral polish. Otherwise, it will change the color of the shoe or boot. To be safe when in doubt use neutral polish for brown shoes and boots.

Brushing the Shoes

First you should lay the small hand washing towel on a flat surface and set your shoes on them. This creates a surface area for any fallen specs of dirt, shoe polish and such to be caught and not damage your floor, table or wherever else you are polishing your shoes.

You want to use your brush to clean any dirt off your shoes. To do this simply remove the laces from your shoes and then brush them.

A proper shoe cleaning brush usually has two sides to its thistles; one black and one that is neutral color. These are for using on black or brown shoes, respectively. Do not use the black side on neutral-colored shoes. As this brush will eventually pick up pieces of the polish from your shoes you do not want to mix the sides up, otherwise you can smear pieces of black shoe polish on your brown shoes.

I should mention here that after you have polished your shoes for the first time, a simple brushing of your shoes after usage will restore a clean crisp look to them without necessarily needing to re-apply any polish to them. Occasionally, when your shoes sit for a long time they can start to build up some white lines along the seams and a simple brushing will dispense with this. It is often enough to avoid your shoes from rotting away to simply brush them when you see white lines appear.

Applying Shoe Polish to your Shoes

You want two polish applicator brushes; one for neutral color paste that can be used on brown shoes, and one for black. You cannot mix these up, as it will ruin your shoes. You will find it nearly impossible to clean a brush that is used for applying shoe polish, so it is better for these to be separate brushes. Applicator brushes are small brushes, somewhat of a similar size as shaving cream applicator brushes yet with more firm bristles.

To begin applying you will scrub a good chunk of polish onto your brush and then smear it on your shoe, covering the whole of it. You should cover the entire exterior of the shoe, tongue and all. Obviously do not put polish on the inside of the shoe where your foot will go and do not apply paste to the bottom of the shoe, either.

After you have applied shoe polish to your shoes you will then place your applicator brush into a zip lock bag. This will prevent the brush from dirtying the rest of your kit. Likewise, you should put your shoe polish into baggies to prevent their contents from spilling out of the cans, as is a common occurrence.

How to Brush Your Shoe Until It Has a Spit Shine Look

Next, take your medium size brush and simply brush the polish in until it has a dull matte look that is evenly spread among the shoe. It is important to do this with the medium size brush and not the brush for cleaning your shoes.

You will then use the heat gun on the low temperature setting to melt the shoe polish on the shoe in a specific area, which quickly manifests as a shiny spot on the shoe. This will happen in just a few seconds of directing heat to the polish.

You will then take some lightly damp cotton balls that have been wetted in some water and then make small circles on the heated area of the shoe. This is how you do a proper military style spit shine.

If you don't want to use cotton balls, you can alternatively use a white napkin or even a piece of torn up t-shirt to buff the melted polish. This will create the same effect.

In the olden days, men would use lighters to heat up a spoon and then apply the spoon to the leather to melt the polish, but this is a far more time-consuming process that can lead to uneven polishing. I recommend you use a heat gun instead.

Now let me explain why you use Lincoln shoe polish instead of Kiwi. Lincoln shoe polish will not easily crack while wearing your shoes. Doing a spit shine with Kiwi wax will often cause cracking, as the wax is of poor quality. I served five years in the military and this is how I always shined my boots for my entire service career; I never once experienced any cracking on my boots while using Lincoln shoe polish to perform a spit shine.

Lincoln shoe polish is often sold at military PXs however if you are a civilian you will need to order them off Amazon. Some specialty shoe stores may carry it but department stores like Walmart typically do not carry anything except Kiwi. With Lincoln shoe polish you will not need to apply anything else to protect your shoes or boots from water, as Lincoln polish is waterproof.

There really isn't more to this process than what I have described. There many other products, oils and gadgets people try to sell to men who are new to shoe polishing and you don't need them.

How to Clean a Suit Jacket

If you are in a suit and have to wear it all day, you might want to consider cleaning it. If you do not clean your suit jacket the oils from your skin will eventually start to break down the fibers of the jacket. Most suit jackets are made from polyester and should be treated with the same care as a dress shirt.

Here's the most important thing that you need to know about how to clean a suit jacket: Machine washing a suit jacket can damage the fibers and make it unwearable. It is better to hand wash your suit jackets to preserve their shape, as well as keep their color bright. When it comes to whether you should have your suit jacket dry cleaned, the answer is yes. Dry cleaning a suit jacket is designed to re-move all traces of dirt and oil from your clothing, so there is no need to wash it again by hand.

There are a lot of different ways to wash a suit jacket, but the best method is to dry clean it. Alternatively, you can hand wash it with a gentle detergent and hang it to dry. You should avoid washing a suit in a washing machine, as this can damage the fabrics.

If you ever find yourself needing to wash a dressy suit, then follow these steps and you will know how to wash suit jackets.

How to Clean a Suit Jacket by Hand

If you want to keep your suit jacket looking new and crisp, you need to keep it clean. The easiest way is to put a bit of white vinegar in a spray bottle and mist that jacket so the dirt and grime comes off easily.

Special care should be taken with wool jackets, as they can easily shrink. It may be better to have a wool jacket dry cleaned, especially if the jacket is very expensive. This method should only be used with cotton or polyester jackets for this reason, and even then, be careful.

- Step 1) Unbutton the jacket.
- Step 2) Turn the jacket inside out.
- Step 3) Gently hand wash the jacket in a tub of cold water.

- Step 4) Hang the jacket to dry at room temperature. Don't expose it to high heat or hang it near a radiator, furnace or other heat source as this will cause the fibers to shrink.

As a general rule, you should never machine wash a suit jacket, especially if there are any kind of plaid or stripes on the jacket. The colors can bleed easily and the threads become damaged.

How to Get a Suit Dry Cleaned

Suit jackets and blazer dry cleaners can work wonders on clothing that's been hanging in the back of your closet for years. You can get an old, dirty, stained blazer looking like it came off the rack at your favorite department store. You can request a free consultation with a dry cleaner near you and see what special services you can get.

Blazer cleaning or pressing can add a year onto the life of a tired, old blazer and give it that professional, like-new look that it deserves. Dry cleaners can often remove tough stain spots and give your garments a new lease on life.

When your schedule has opened up to give you time to go to a dry cleaner, you can pick up the phone and get your suit jacket and pants cleaned by a professional dry cleaner located near you, that specializes in quality dry cleaning. This way you can ask how long it will take to have the dry cleaning done ahead of time, and choose a location that is able to get your suit cleaned the fastest. You can also ensure the dry cleaner is still in business; sometimes defunct dry cleaner locations are still listed on Yelp and it can save you a trip to call ahead and make sure they are still in business.

Can a Suit be Dry Cleaned in a Day?

A suit can be dry cleaned in a day, but it will depend largely on what time of day you take the suit to the dry cleaner. They must have enough time in the day to be able to clean the suit in addition to all of the other customer orders for dry cleaning that they have received. While we'd all like to think that our suits and shirts can be dry cleaned in a day, the reality is they can sometimes take a little longer.

It's best to take your suit to a dry cleaner as soon as possible when you know you need to have it cleaned. And don't try to wash it with your regular laundry detergent at home, or you can damage its fibers.

General Advice for Taking Care

of Your Health

In addition to all the previous advice I have provided on nutrition, exercise and diet, here are some additional tips that will help you ensure you take care of your body and extend the longevity of your health.

1. Do not listen to excessively loud music and rarely attend concerts where excessively loud music plays, unless you wear ear plugs. Do not wear noise-canceling headphones for long periods of time exceeding two hours. The noise-canceling feature causes tinnitus, often within two years. Tinnitus is an extremely painful ringing in your ear as your eardrum organ fails. It can make a person go mad and should be avoided. Take care of your ears.

2. Do not stare directly at the sun, even while wearing sunglasses, or you will permanently damage your eyes. Do not stare directly at any other exceptionally bright light directly, such as a welding torch or lasers, without proper protective eyewear. The damage to the eyes will cause permanent and irreversible blindless. Likewise, do not spend many hours of time

watching television or computer monitors in the dark. This, too, can damage the eyes permanently.

3. Avoid engaging in excessively dangerous stunts, such as bungee jumping off bridges and sky diving, unless it serves a necessary purpose, such as part of military operations. While many people do not die from these, many people do. You could be one of the ones who experience a malfunction of equipment and die. Someone always is. It is often better to be accused of being a coward by peers instead of being thought a brave fool who died trying to impress someone.

4. Brush your teeth at least once a day. Avoid using whitening staining toothpaste, as this damages your enamel. Use toothpicks to dislodge any food that is stuck between your tooth, for lodged food between the teeth and gums becomes acidic to teeth and creates cavities and infections.

5. Shower or bath at least once a day. This will prevent harmful bacteria from growing on your body, leading to infections.

6. When using public showers, such as at campgrounds or gyms, always wear cheap sandals. This will reduce your chance of getting a fungal infection on the bottom of your feet. While not fatal, they are painful and annoying to kill. If you develop a plantar wart on the bottom of your foot, the best way to kill it is by applying a small amount of salicylic acid to the wart and then wrap the area with duct tape for a week. This is effective because plantar warts gain oxygen

from the blood flowing in nearby skin cells and wrapping the surface of the foot with duct tape will cause skin on the surface to die. After a week you can peel away the dead layers of skin and the plantar wart using a pumice stone and some toenail clippers.

7. Do not allow trash to pile up in your home. This will attract pests such as rodents and insects, who bring disease. The garbage itself can foster harmful bacteria and disease as well, which you will breathe in and become infected by. Always take out your trash at least once a week and make sure you do not allow dirty dishes to sit around for longer than a few days. Always clean your dishes using soap and water, ideally hot water.

8. Never drink water that has not been purified, filtered or boiled. Do not drink water directly from puddles, lakes, streams or wells – it must be treated to be safe. Drinking water directly from such places without any treatment of the water will cause you to become infected with parasites and viruses that live in these sources of water. Because present day micro-organisms have evolved for hundreds of thousands of years, they are much nastier than the kinds which our ancestors had to deal with – present-day parasites and viruses are more lethal to humans today than in the past. Wild animals frequently get infected by drinking water from these sources, which is also why pets such as dogs and cats often get these infections and then require treatment. Always make sure you drink water that has been purified filtered or boiled.

9. Avoid using hallucinogenic drugs. I have lost once close friends in my life as a consequence of their addictions robbing them of their sanity. These drugs tend to damage the mind and make it more difficult to control your emotions and think logically. Many of these drugs will permanently damage your mind and cause mental illness. If you feel sad, depressed, or bored, there are better solutions to improve your situation than being using drugs. Address the problems in your life that are making you feel disenfranchised with life, and you will have no need for these drugs. Focus on becoming an excellent person.

10. Do not excessively drink alcohol. Alcohol is water-soluble and the human liver has adapted to filter it out of our bodies, as our ancestors primarily used alcohol to treat water for long-term storage and make it safe for drinking. However, consuming alcohol in large doses, such as with binge drinking, will cause poisoning and death, and damage the liver to where it cannot function anymore. Hospitals frequently refuse to perform liver transplants for alcoholics, on the belief they will just keep drinking themselves to death. Several people in my life have died this way, including close friends and family. Heed my advice. Stop drinking when you feel very disoriented and do not drink to the point that you feel sickly. If you are vomiting from drinking, it means your blood alcohol level is at lethal levels that your liver cannot process, and your body is purging alcohol from your stomach

in an effort to avoid death. Immediately stop drinking alcohol and consume water instead, ideally water with electrolytes in it. Water and electrolytes to recover lost fluids from vomiting and time for your liver to restore your proper blood levels is the only thing that can recover from drunkenness. Do not drink caffeinated beverages, as this only gives the perception of improvement and caffeine while drunk will impair health. Don't drink caffeine when your body is experiencing a medical emergency event such as purging alcohol from its system. The only cure for drunkenness is water, electrolytes and rest.

11. Do not allow the idea of having sex, the pursuit of sexual pleasure and your excitement of sexual fetishes, to become the primary purpose of your life and a critical aspect of your personal identity. The pursuit of carnal pleasures in the absence of virtue frequently leads to madness of the mind and distraction from worthier pursuits. Sex can be fun and enjoyable, but it can also be an addiction that distracts a person from what is truly important in life. This addiction will not fill the empty void of the human heart. You can only best fill that void with the pursuit of excellence.

12. Try to keep company with good people who share the values outlined in this book. If you keep company with people who do not share the values, it is likely you will become more like them and less than how you wish to be. This is because behavioral mimicry is instinctive to humans. Associate yourself with

people you wish to be more like and who wish to be more like how you wish to be.

13. Always remember that every day, the choices you make determine the person that you are. If you make choices of low moral character, then you become a person of low morality; if you make choices of high moral character then you become a person of high morality. You and only you, can decide what kind of person of character you will be, and you make this decision every day of your life in the actions you choose to do.

14. Try to make the most of the hours of your life. You only have a finite number of them. When we are young, it feels like we have all of the time in the world, but Time is constantly moving forward, ticking away with every breath we breathe. There is only a finite number of sunrises and sunsets a person can experience in life, and the Time that is lost can never be recovered. There are choices made that can never be undone, and untreaded paths that can never be walked. There is no such thing as a stand-still in life; Time is always moving forward, and so we too are with it, always moving forward. Employ your Time wisely, make the most of it, achieve what you can with the Time that you have. If you squander your Time, you can never go back and make different choices. One day, you will die, and no one and nothing can change that. The question you must answer is, how will you live with the Time you possess while you are alive? Your actions are your answer.

On Building Wealth

'Those who approach life like a child play a game, moving and pushing pieces, possess the power of kings.'
- Heraclitus, ancient Greek philosopher

As a young man you must search out adventure in your life; you cannot lie in wait and expect that adventures will come to you. Now, there are three great types of adventures in this world; the first is military service, the second is exploration of unknown lands and places, and the third is entrepreneurship. This section we will talk about the latter, and in another we will discuss the other two.

Acquiring wealth is a game of markets, and an adventure in and of itself. Enterprise itself is a great and rewarding adventure and if you desire to acquire societal power, the most direct way to achieve this.

I advise that you should focus on acquiring generational wealth more than personal indulgence. This means establishing reliable cash flows that do not expressly rely on you or someone in your family to be actively working; examples of assets that can produce reliable passive cash flow are patents, creative works such as books, paintings or music, leased real estate, and dividends from stocks, mutual funds and exchange traded funds. These assets must also be correctly protected with corporate structure that reduce tax obligations and allow them to be passed to heirs while avoiding inheritance taxes as much as possible. While many people will not be able to build vast fortunes within their lifetimes, through generations of the family estate managed correctly by yourself and your heirs, a large fortune can be developed that will provide for your descendants and ensure the longevity of your family lineage. As the Greek proverb goes, "A society grows great when old men plant trees in whose shade they shall never sit."

When we are young, we often feel we have all the time in the world, but it is actually quite short. Days feel longer when we are busy and when we are idle, we lose it quicker. Regardless of how slow or quick we feel it pass us by; time is precious and we cannot get back any of the time that has been spent. So, spend your time wisely and fruit- fully, toward things that will help you acquire wealth. Even if you are a child this is true, because much of your time should be spent educating yourself on how to obtain wealth as an adult. If you are a quick enough learner you may dis- cover you can even begin obtaining wealth as a teenager.

The acquisition of an ancestral home to serve as shel- ter and training ground for raising children who are stable, sane, cultured, intelligent and strong. Depending on your current social and economic status, it may take you many years, even decades to acquire a property that is suitable to be regarded as an ancestral home but acquiring the wealth to do so should be your primary concern. The task can be so difficult that it may be the only thing you truly accomplish in your life and if so, that is sufficient.

Most homes are unsuitable to be regarded as an ancestral home. They are poorly constructed, are part of homeowner associations that can seize your home under certain conditions, and have restrictions on using the home as a source of revenue generation which is vital. An ancestral home must be an estate; it must be a place with enough acreage to accommodate at least an orchard field, or other farming lot such as the growing of grapes for wine or some such. The land itself must produce revenue to cover the property taxes of the property. This is the great failure of many people who purchase land; they do not understand that the home becomes a depreciable asset if you cannot use it to produce revenue directly. At some point you may lose your occupation or the property taxes increase due to other development of the area, and maintaining the home will be unsuitable for you or future generations if the estate itself does not produce revenue to cover its own upkeep and taxes. My grandparent's farm where I was raised in my youth was ideal for an ancestral home estate and I wish my family had kept it instead of selling it; contrast this to my mother who has spent her adult life purchasing many homes across the country, none of which produce any revenue and which she loses money on.

Once an ancestral home has been acquired, expansion and development of it to enhance opportunities for cultivating children and obtaining new income should also be focused on. Your heirs must be instructed on how to govern the estate. While it is tempting in many families to distribute inheritance over all children equally, this is not wise. Wealthy families wishing to maintain their social status instead will raise one child expressly to inherit the responsibility of governing over the family wealth and the other offspring will instead receive dividends from the property portfolio of the family estate; ideally the unappointed heirs will use their education to build their own successful businesses and potential ancestral homes, so that should an appointed heir make poor choices one of the other branch families can pick up the slack and take over governance after purchasing the original estate from the incompetent heir governor. The greatest failure that has brought down once prominent families is only picking one heir to govern the estate and then not teaching the other children anything so they could not be successful in their own lives and compensate for any mistakes the appointed heir may make.

Without a well-planned system for inheritance that takes full advantage of tax and estate laws your heirs will lose their fortune within a few generations and likely never recover it. You must plan several generations ahead and raise a successor who can modify the plan wisely as events unfold.

The means to obtain wealth is largely in developing passive income streams. It can sometimes be necessary to build an income stream that requires you to scale it but eventually if successful you can afford to hire someone to replace you in the management of the business which will turn it into a passive income stream.

If you wish to get into retail the ideal method of doing so is not to invest into stocks of inventory with your own money but instead by working on consignment of others products and focus on the marketing and selling of the product or service. You can do this with several means such as drop shipping from the supplier. Once you have developed a reputation as a merchant and have reliable sales coming in you can increase your profit margins and scale by investing your profits into purchasing products wholesale, or even in manufacturing goods yourself. But you should first develop the sales channel to sell products before you purchase stock and before you manufacture goods. This greatly lowers your risk of losing the capital spent to acquire stock of products to sell.

Another commonplace mistake, especially among the middle class and poor, is the belief by parents that children should learn to build wealth entirely on their own and grow that wealth. The parents often feel exceptionally possessive of the property and things they acquire with money they earned and do not view these assets as liquid in nature, and that their primary duty is to raise children. The act of raising children becomes secondary to their lives, and their first primary objective is indulgences of their lives. This is flawed and makes it exceptionally more difficult to build generational wealth, as each generation becomes expected to build a fortune anew instead of wealth being viewed as a generational asset that should be used to benefit the family as a whole. Part of the reason this attitude has developed is because divorce has become so widespread, so it becomes difficult to view wealth generationally when a wife takes half the assets of the father and does what she wants with another new husband. This is also why it is so important for you as a young man to not rush into marriage and to pick a wife who has the necessary qualities for a stable marriage that will not lead to divorce and allows for the cultivation of generational wealth -- most importantly through her contribution as a mother that raises stable, healthy children. This is discussed in more detail later in this book.

Another factor that is necessary for the acquisition of wealth is to belong to communities of likeminded entrepreneurial people. You must cultivate and maintain a network of others of similar social status which can serve to create new opportunities for business growth. If you are a penniless entrepreneur you will be unable to just waltz into a community of millionaires, however you can network with other small business owners and grow your opportunities that way. This is also why it is necessary to develop the social qualities so that you can employ charm to win over new allies.

Technology is always among the best ventures to focus your efforts of wealth generation into. While revenue is generated in traditional ways even today, such as direct retail and through trading your manual labor for money, technology has the largest opportunity for wealth generation at all times. Anything that solves a critical problem for people that reduces the expense of solving the problem is a technology business opportunity, usually by reducing layers of complexity necessary to solve the problem.

Business structures that should always be avoided are multi-level marketing schemes. Investments into stocks and other high-risk ventures should only be done with a small portion of disposable income, and only after passive income revenue streams have been setup that produce reliable income. Passive income is always better than income obtained from employment, as you can lose employment any number of ways, especially if you experience injury. Passive income does not depend upon such factors, requiring far less maintenance to keep the money flowing.

To finish out this section of general advice on wealth acquisition and retainment for your family, never under any circumstances give someone, even a friend or family member, general power of attorney over you. Many men have made the mistake of doing this during some kind of emergency, such as deployment overseas during military service, and came back to discover their wife signing their name on divorce documents and depleting their bank accounts while awarding themselves full custody of his children. This is just one example of things that can occur. At the most, only specialized power of attorney agreements for specific types of business and affairs should be signed for certain things. Always consult with an attorney about these issues and never give an attorney general power of attorney over your affairs, either.

Using Permanent Life Insurance Policies as an Asset

Many types of asset strategies depend largely on current regulations and market fluctuations and if I tried to give you specific advice on many things such as mutual funds or annuity on retirement accounts, the advice would be unlikely to age well. However, there is one kind of instrument which is largely immune to change and very low risk, and that is the use of permanent life insurance policies as an asset.

Many people do not fully understand the value of life insurance policies as an asset, and this is because term insurance policies have become the present standard so that is what most people are familiar with. This is because many people obtain term insurance policies through their employers or when also purchasing insurance for their cars, and this term insurance system primarily benefits the insurance companies as many people will never be paid out for lack of an accident with that car or experiencing death during employment and having that policy. However, the very wealthy understand that other kinds of insurance policies such as whole life insurance (also called permanent life insurance) can serve multiple purposes and be treated as an investment strategy.

The main drawback of term life insurance is that the policy is not an asset; it is only applicable in the event of your death and until your death, it is an expense. You also lose the benefits if you stop making the premium payments, for whatever reason. The benefits for a term life insurance policy are only for covering your burial costs and providing some income for your heirs.

In contrast to a term life insurance policy, a whole life insurance policy carries with it a cash value account that you can borrow against or that can even be used as an asset for leveraging loans. By overpaying the premium, excess money is credited to the cash value account as if it was a deposit into a savings account. Unlike savings accounts, the cash value account of a whole life insurance policy is tax deferred, yet similar to a savings account it carries an interest rate on the cash that accumulates in the account from your payments. This means the larger its fund the more the cash value account can grow from that interest rate. You can also make a withdrawal of the cash value as well, which decreases your coverage amount at death and will be taxed, but due to this instrument's value as an asset, as a long-term strategy this can be more intelligent even if the payments are more expensive than term life insurance is. Lastly the payments of a whole life insurance are fixed and will not increase over time unlike a term policy will, and the interest rate on the cash value account is also fixed. This protects the account against the changes of market fluctuations, so unlike a normal bank account where (due to inflation) the money becomes less valuable (in terms of purchasing power) the longer it sits inside a conventional bank savings account, the untaxed returns of money in a life insurance policy's cash value account can actually be retained or even increase due to the interest rate.

(This is not to suggest that conventional bank savings accounts are useless, because they are not. Their primary value is security and control; it is difficult for the money to be stolen from you and due to regulatory required insurance, you cannot lose the money in the event of a market crash. However, the fact remains that the purchasing power of money in an account decreases as inflation of the currency occurs and inflation is always occurring, especially as you are taxed on any accrued interest in these savings accounts).

As part of inheritance planning, many wealthy families frequently take out a whole life insurance policy for their children at the time they are born so that by the time the child is an adult the cash value account can be used by the child as an asset for obtaining a loan. The advantage of this is that because the cash value account represents actual money, there is no credit requirement to obtain such a loan. Best of all if you never withdraw the capital and only loan against it, this means you never pay taxes on any of the money that accumulates in the account. The money in the cash value account can also be used to make the premium payments on the policy itself, which means the accrued interest on the cash value account could potentially pay the premiums when the account is old enough, which seems to generally be when the account is a decade old.

So, the best way to think about this kind of life insurance policy is that it is like a bank savings account that has a

162

death benefit associated with it. If you pay into it enough your death benefit can pay out millions of dollars to your beneficiary while giving you a cash value account during your lifetime that can be used like a savings account, to be borrowed against when you need to obtain loans or withdrawn from in emergencies. As an asset for loans, you could borrow against the cash value of the life insurance policy account to obtain a loan for purchasing real estate which can then be rented out, and you can pay back the loan using cash flow from the rental. This means the cash value of the account never decreases and continues to accrue tax free interest each year, so the account compounds even though you have a loan against that asset.

This is a sophisticated strategy many wealthy families use, compared to the savings deposit strategy many non-sophisticated real estate investors use that is commonly encouraged in most real estate developer 'entrepreneur' books, where you pay cash to purchase properties instead of leveraging assets (such as a life insurance policy) whose cash gains from accrued interest may exceed the accrued interest debt of the loan to purchase the property. This is particularly effective if you plan to flip real estate properties.

When selecting a lifetime insurance policy like this you must ensure it carries a rider that allows both the death benefit and the cash value account to also be paid to the beneficiary; otherwise, the cash value of the account will be absorbed by the insurance provider and only the death benefit of the policy will be paid to a beneficiary. You should also look into riders that provide accelerated benefits, such as allowing an early payout on death benefits if you become diagnosed with a chronic or terminal illness so that some of the money can be used to help pay for medical care at your end of life.

As each policy is going to be different, I will not provide you specific information on how to best structure the policy. This is something you should go over with an accountant. My goal here is to bring this strategy to your awareness.

Due to a whole life insurance policy's value as a long-term financial strategy instrument, this strategy is less useful for elderly people but is intelligent for younger people who can tap into the cash value account to handle emergencies, for launching new businesses or other ventures. This strategy will also not produce as high of a return on investment money as many other kinds of strategies have the potential to do, but this is one of the most secure ways with the least amount of risk. This is especially true because the locked-in interest rate and premium payment prices of the policy will not rise as the value of a dollar inflates, which it inevitably always does. So, with a lifetime policy the full benefits only material after several years and they certainly do after the child is eighteen years old and will persist with them for the remainder of their lives. Indeed, the accrued money of the cash value account of a deceased parent's life insurance policy can be used to open new policies for the beneficiary's children. This is a strategy for generational wealth accruement, which is why many people today in my generation do not fully appreciate this strategy. They do not think of wealth in generational terms as I am advising you to do here.

Using the Pareto Principle for Wealth and Relationships Planning

Many people are interested in life hacks for increasing productivity and maximizing their return on time investment into activities. Everyone wants to be more successful in life so it's common to seek out information on how to change one or two things to make yourself more successful. If that is the kind of tips and advice you're looking for, I will introduce you to the 80/20 Rule, also referred to as the Pareto Principle.

What is the 80/20 Rule?

In the 19th century Italian philosopher and economist Vilfredo Federico Damaso Pareto developed the 80/20 Rule based on observations he made in his garden; he noticed that 20% of his pea pods produced the majority of the peas in his garden. He then started looking at other things such as wealth distribution and land ownership, and discovered that 20% of the population in Italy owned most of the land and possessed most of the wealth. This developed into what is referred to as the Pareto Principle, which is an aphorism (an observation that contains a general truth). While this is not a hard science, generally speaking in any group you'll find roughly 20% of that group is responsible for 80% of the utility of that group.

As an example, let's take your wardrobe. Chances are that while you may own many clothes, roughly 20% of your clothing is actually worn regularly by you. You'll often wear the same shoes, pants, shirts and coats even if you own a variety of them. This is because some clothes just have more general utility than others — I rarely dress in my formal attire because they are for special occasions and events. Most of the time I wear my Lucky brand jeans and a black t-shirt.

If you'd like more proof this is relevant to you, consider your phone app; you probably don't use the majority of the apps on your phone, right? Only around 20% of them get used frequently by you and are responsible for at least 80% of your monthly bandwidth usage.

The 80/20 rule is also applicable to dating; if you are using an online app, you'll find that somewhere around 20% of the women you message will reply to you. Likewise, a low percentage (like 20%) of the women on the dating service are receiving the bulk of the messages as these are the most attractive and desirable ones.

In business, the 80/20 rule usually turns out to be that 20% of your customers are responsible for 80% of your income — a good example of this is with any kind of micro-transaction business model, such as in gaming. Whales spend far more than the majority of the playerbase does, and make up for the lack of purchases made by other free players. You can also find that 20% of the work a company does can be responsible for 80% of the revenue it generates — this tends to lead to downsizing inside companies that expand too quickly. In an ideal world all employees would contribute equally to the company but that's just not how it works in practice — you always end up with A team players and B team players in your employee roster, and eventually you have to lay off or even fire the underperforming employees because they aren't pulling their own weight.

How to Take Advantage of the Pareto Principle 80/20 Rule to Succeed in Life

The 80/20 Rule, or Pareto Principle, is very useful for improvising productivity and time management. It helps a person realize they can focus on the most productive tasks and reduce the time you spend on less productive ones.

As a personal example (that is likely very relatable to many men) I used to spend a lot of time playing online MMORPG videogames *like Nexus: The Kingdom of the Winds, World of Warcraft, Ragnarok Online* and *Final Fantasy XIV*. I was a huge gamer back in my youth — so passionate about it that my most well-known YouTube channel was devoted to playing roleplaying videogames. Yet when I looked at what activities in my life helped me make the most money and therefore increased the quality of my life, playing videogames just wasn't that productive for me personally. While some people find that playing videogames helps them launch a very successful career as a Twitch or YouTube creator, it wasn't working out that way for me personally. While I gained millions of views and over 15,000 subscribers to my personal channel, the majority of my income was revenue from video production gigs I did for local businesses when I filmed a commercial for them, as well as revenue from affiliate links on various blogs I owned. Realizing this, I started looking at how I could leverage these skills to produce more revenue and I gravitated toward starting a YouTube multi-channel network.

As another business example, with my blogs it tends to be that somewhere around 20% of the articles are responsible for 80% of the visits — the majority of articles don't generate the bulk of the traffic. Understanding which topics generate the most interest and writing more articles about those topics helps me create more articles that will produce more revenue for my blogs.

By following the Pareto Principle you can spend less time on trivial and unimportant activities that don't help you achieve the goals you are striving for, increasing your productivity.

On Cultivating Your Mind Through Education

It is necessary for your success in life that you develop a healthy passion for the pursuit of knowledge. This is because knowledge is necessary to become virtuous and virtue is necessary to attain happiness. This is one of the foundations of the Socratic theory of knowledge and this forms an important basis for much of Western philosophy, a subject which you must master if you are to become a gentleman.

Although many past philosophers were mistaken in many things (including Socrates) the best of their contributions to the field have made way for modern philosophies, including the Chivalric Humanism of my own construction. It is necessary to study the chronological development of philosophical ideas if you are to truly understand history and how the ideologies of past generations shaped their communities, and contributed to the development of the present state of human affairs. It is impossible to fully appreciate and understand the present if you do not understand this history, and so you must study philosophers of all kinds and understand their points of view, if you are to truly understand human history.

Lastly you must also read fictional works, especially the most significant ones whose ideas have influenced populist movements. Without having done this you cannot understand them and many of these populist movements from the past are still with us today in fragmented forms, but many people who advocate these ideas do not know from whence these ideas originated and what the goals of their originators were. For example, many people learn about the psychological experiments and theories of B.F. Skinner regarding operational conditioning but because they do not read his fiction, such as *Walden Two*, they do not understand how he intended his ideas to be applied in society and see that he was unrealistically optimistic about how these ideas would be implemented. By contrast Aldous Huxley's *Brave New World* has been demonstrated to have been a more realistic portrayal of what kind of society B.F. Skinner's ideas would lead to, as the present society is one where people want to trade their liberties for pleasure and comfort; the masses are choosing indulgence in psycho-active drugs, gaming world, junk food, instant sexual gratification and other hedonism. They sacrifice their health, their minds and their freedom to instead become loyal consumers of commercial brands and political movements that do not serve their own long-term interests whatsoever. The only way that a man can safeguard himself from the same mistaken path that leads to pleasurable servitude (that inevitably ends in regret and tragedy) is to be well educated so that he can recognize the manipulative efforts and reject them before they can take root in his mind and condition him to be a happy idiot.

As the ex-slave and American abolitionist leader Frederick Douglass wrote in his autobiography,
"I have found that, to make a contented slave, it is necessary to make a thoughtless one...He must be able to detect no inconsistencies in slavery; he must be made to feel

that slavery is right; and he can be brought to that only when he ceases to be a man."

This is not to suggest you should be a jack of all trades and master of none when it comes to educating yourself and learning skills. Although I prescribe study in a wide degree of necessary subjects, you must ultimately select a vocation for your life, whose skills you should master. The path of least resistance is usually the best when it comes to selecting your vocation and focusing your efforts on achieving goals. Therefore, you should cultivate your natural gifts. Passion is indicative of a potential gift, even if the talent is not noticeable at first. Unless you intend to work in academia you probably do not need a doctorate degree. What you really need are valuable skills so you can work a trade that is well compensated by those who do not have those skills and will pay you for your employment of them.

This said do not avoid everything just because it is challenging at first. Humans are rarely instinctively good at subjects such as mathematics and only a lucky few have the natural predisposition for it. Still, the basics of arithmetic are so critical to success in our world that if you do not understand mathematics you cannot make much of yourself. Personally speaking, I have possessed a form of dyscalculia for all of my life; I completely lack the ability to do arithmetic in my mind, so mental math is impossible for me. Yet I have still learned the rules to how math is performed and have learned tricks to enable me to do math when I need to. I am also not so prideful as to not take out a calculator just to be able to calculate tips when I pay a bill; this is the reality of my disability and you cannot navigate a life successfully if you cannot be realistic about those things you need help doing. And although a calculator is a tool that will do calculations for me, I still must know what algorithm is best to employ in any situation. This requires learning the rules of mathematics and no disability is an excuse for you, as a young man, to not learn it because this subject is too critical to the success of your life.

Education is more than just the memorization of facts. It is also the ability to weave these facts into a useful tapestry; to apply your knowledge to developing and implementing solutions to problems.

The most important things to learn are mathematics and the study of logic, modern languages, rhetoric and debate, the natural sciences of physics and biology, to study world histories, knowledge of the laws of your country (especially those laws which pertain to operating a business) and master the usage of computers. You should also develop mastery of the body through cultivation of your physique, which I have written about in a previous section. Education in these matters ideally will begin at age seven.

If you cannot develop competence in these areas it will be near impossible for you to build generational wealth; you could win a lottery and be awarded millions, but you will quickly squander it if you do not have a full education in these aforementioned subjects because you will lack the knowledge necessary to invest that money wisely. This is partly because you will be highly susceptible to scammers who will take advantage of your ignorance to trick you in many ways but it is also because you will not know how to invest the money into ventures that will produce profits.

It is also exceptionally valuable to know how to research the answers to questions which others have, which comes from practice in researching how to answer your own questions.

I will encourage you to try to learn Latin. Latin was once part of Western classical education but has become rare in our age. It has since primarily been a subject taught to college students as part of either a History, Law or Medical degree program, as these professions frequently require knowledge of Latin. I believe this approach is wrong and that all children who speak English would benefit from learning Latin. This is because Latin composes 60% of all modern English words, as the form of English we use today is a combination of medieval English and Latin.

Latin is necessary in order to read many of the classical works of literature and philosophy in their original untranslated forms, which is useful for fully understanding these works that influenced the development of America.

Latin is also a foundation for logic itself. The Latin language is the basis of logic and so it is also the basis of mathematics. By learning Latin a child can better understand the structure of mathematical logic, as mathematics is itself a language that organizes itself according to logic. So by one learning Latin (which is a logic ordered language) then a child can better understand mathematics.

Once a person understands Latin it becomes easier for understanding many other languages, because to learn Latin when you first know modern English requires learning how to break down a language to its grammatical structure and understand how to form sentences using it. Learning Latin therefore helps an English-speaking child later learn Spanish, French, Italian, Portuguese, and so on.

At the back of this book will be a list of Recommended Reading. These are books which I believe all young men should read before they are eighteen years old. You need not read them all at once, but you should be able to read and understand their contents by the time you are eighteen.

Do not expect the state factory school system to supply you with a curriculum to learn these subjects in the necessary amount of detail as to be well versed in them; this is a common trap. The public education system is designed to serve the lowest common denominator. It is not designed to raise children into philosophers or men of letters, orators, poets or great artists. The systems are not designed to produce boys into gentlemen, and this is why they fail at accomplishing such. The truth is that for many subjects, the classroom is a slow place to learn about many subjects; for example, you can learn all the most important details of human history in a month of dedicating yourself a Saturday and Sunday of reading, if you choose the correct books. This is true for many subjects.

You must take charge of your own education and that of your children when you are a man, to ensure the subjects I prescribed are studied comprehensively. When I was a child in grade school I spent my recesses in the school library until I had read every book of both fiction and non-fiction. Then I would sneak away during recess to the city public library across the street and read more complex topics. I particularly loved reading encyclopedias and dictionaries for their ability to greatly expand vocabulary and subject knowledge in a short amount of time. I recommend that you invest your time during your youth wisely, and if you are a parent where the public school system is particularly failing you may consider removing your child from it and sending them to either a private institute or hiring a live-in tutor if you have the means to assist with the education of the children.

On the subject of a live-in tutor, this is one of the benefits of obtaining generational wealth and a family estate, so that you can afford to do this and ensure your children receive a proper education in these matters which the public school system simply will not provide. If you do not have the wealth to provide specialized education to your child by means of a tutor or private school then you must at the very least encourage them to spend time at the local libraries reading anything and everything that interests them. I would suggest they at least spend a Sunday at the local library for part of the school year becoming introduced to books they may not otherwise have discovered were the book not immediately before them.

It is also good to remember that even reputable education programs can be predatory, convincing students to pay for expensive classes that are not strictly necessary nor useful, but which they may claim are valuable in intangible ways. Regardless of whether it is a university or an internet-based course, be cautious of paying thousands of dollars for classes that will not directly lead to you producing wealth.

Even if you fail at things you try to achieve you must at least pass on the wisdom that you have acquired from those failures to the next generation so that they might be better prepared to accomplish those things that you could not. This is the duty of every man.

A word of caution regarding your indulgence in amusements; do not make the ambition of your life a hobby. It is fine to possess interests and passions, but the purpose of your life is not to collect idle useless things such as plastic dolls of popular literary characters such as from comic books and movies, or large stockpiles of games you may rarely play, or other kinds of memorabilia. These things can have monetary value but it varies at times depending on the wealth of those who are collecting it. You must avoid becoming a hoarder of junk out of boredom for not knowing what to do with your life. The easiest way to avoid this is to ensure your collection has a purpose that is relevant to the acquisition of generational wealth for your family and the education of progeny. For example, it is fine to collect books which will provide an education not only for yourself, but for your children and their heirs as part of a large literary collection in a personal family library, or because you are a book seller or publisher who requires vast amounts of literary knowledge of many genres to do your career well. Yet, it is not okay to collect books simply because you think it makes you novel or seem intelligent, as this may lead to the collecting of books of little real value.

Do well to remember the words of Philip Dormer Stanhope, 4th Earl of Chesterfield,

"Pleasure is the rock which most young people split upon: they launch out with crowded sails in quest of it, but without a compass to direct their course, or reason sufficient to steer the vessel; for want of which, pain and shame, instead of pleasure, are the returns of their voyage."

On Developing Good Relations with Others

Good relations with others is necessary for prosperity in life, unless you wish to retreat into the woods and live alone. Some people idealize living as a hermit until they experience what that life is really like for themselves. In the end humans are tribal and we are happiest when we are in the company of others whom we can regard as belonging to our tribe.

Good relations with others is necessary for a gentleman, and for raising your social class. Power is often viewed by many today as something a person possesses individually but power is actually a matter of expression. As humans are very tribal creatures, the power of a tribe will always overwhelm the power of any single individual. This means the truly powerful are those who can influence others the most. Power is viewed as synonymous with money but this is only due to the capacity of money to influence others by purchasing of their services and resources. People can be influenced in many ways that do not require the expenditure of money at all, and if you can wield influence well enough, you can acquire a resource such as money in large quantities without having to spend any of your own. This is an important aspect of fundraising for a commercial venture that most people do not understand, which is why the common man views money as something he can only obtain by working for an employer. By contrast, the families of high status have mastered the ability to wield influence and teach this skill to their young. So too must you learn to do this and teach it to your own children.

As a young man you should select as your friends those who share a passion for learning the subjects I have mentioned before, as well as those who share passion for developing the physique of the body; do not fill your circle of friends with boys focused entirely on one or the other. These days you will rarely find a single individual who has a passion for all of this and so you must expect to have certain friends who share some, but not all, your passions and divide the time you spend in their company intelligently if you are unable to organize them into a common group of friends, which is more ideal as it will teach you the steps on how to become a leader of a diverse group of men. To make this work you must learn to view your circle of friends as a network of individuals you are associated with, and whom you can introduce to one another in order to both expand the value of your social network and take the mantle of the role as a leader of men who can bring them together. Children often do this organization accidentally, organizing themselves by popularity of different children as leaders but any boy can become popular if he learns how to make introductions between different children to expand their social friendships, with himself as the common link between them all.

For deciding how to recruit a friend, the simplest way is to solve a problem; most children form friendships to solve each other's problem of needing a playmate to stave off boredom, or a confidence to rely upon. But there are other ways to solve another child's problems. By learning to aid a child of your own age in solving a problem you can learn how to recruit friends and gain trust, which gives you a degree of influence over them. You can then use your network of friends to make introductions as needed to solve other potential friend's problems; for example, if you know someone who is struggling with a math assignment you may have a friend who is excellent at math that is willing to assist that child if you asked him to do so, thereby now recruiting the struggling math child into your network of friends. The child bad at math may have some other thing he is good at or some resource he has access to, and by befriending him you gain access to his circle of friends, too. This allows great expansion of your social network and if you are skilled enough at this you could potentially befriend everyone in your school through all of your grades, and be the natural choice for the most popular boy at school. Accomplishing this can be useful as you will have learned to grow a social network and influence others through positive achievements, and not through tyranny as most boys try to do. As an adult it will greatly benefit you to have this degree of social influence as you will have people to rely upon as you encounter problems in life, but also able to now recruit many other people to your aid and causes throughout your life.

You should also ensure that you do not stockpile garbage in your room, home or otherwise some other location. In addition to attracting pests such as ants, rats and roaches it breeds harmful bacteria that will lead to disease. Garbage also gives a foul odour from the collection of this harmful bacteria which turns people away from you. If your home smells like garbage others will look upon you as garbage yourself. You should dispose of garbage correctly in the proper garbage deposit locations for it to be collected and not litter to make your garbage become someone else's problem, as this breeds hostility toward you from others in addition to that many people may not pick up your garbage, which will attract pests and disease, as mentioned before. If everyone was to throw their garbage on the ground the world would be a dirty unhealthy place, so it is important to learn to do your part toward creating a good clean city for you and everyone else. Walt Disney himself would wander around his theme park Disneyland, snatching up any garbage he saw deposited on the ground to set an example for his employees and other park guests that even the king of a magic kingdom must do his share to keep the kingdom clean.

Endeavor as much as you can to keep company with people above your social station for in their network you can rise but be mindful to not be deemed as a servant to their causes alone. Choose to network with those who have the necessary merits that will color you in good light for you are viewed by others as the company that you keep. A person also has a habit of becoming similar in personality to the types of people they keep in their company.

Sentiments of gratitude toward others are nowadays not common and always appreciated. It is necessary to send thank you cards, and holiday cards as well, to maintain good relationships with others and remind them of your presence in their lives. Once you are married this is something your wife is best left to manage for your personal relationships, but for business acquaintances you must draft and sign the letters yourself.

Concerning your wardrobe and what to wear for in-teractions with others, you must come to appreciate the importance of dressing well. Humans primarily navigate the world and obtain information using our eyes and we largely abide by various rules that stem from pattern recognition. A person who associates a man who is groomed and dressed a certain way will therefore tend to associate another who is groomed and dressed the same way as belonging to a similar social class and tribal group as the first. By wearing the clothing that is associated with wealth and status, you too will be associated with such things. This is the same way that a man dressed in a military uniform is assumed to be a military man; you too must have your own 'uniforms' you wear for certain occasions to project the values you wish others to impart you with. You can of course, through ne-glectful actions, dispel the facade by behaving unruly and inappropriate regardless of how fine your clothing is but without such clothing, no matter how graceful and eloquent you may be, you will not be viewed as a gentleman unless you wear the uniform of one. Always bear this in mind. If you dress and behave noble, then you will be viewed by others as noble.

Do not become so seduced by what is fashionable that you become distracted from those things which are critically important for the duty of your life. When you are young it is tempting to give in to what provides the most instant gratification, but instant gratification often has a toll that must be paid later. Choose your pleasures for yourself and do not have them forced upon you, and be sparing in your indulgences, else you lose your fortune and any chance of building a new one as you become weighed down in the consequences of your short-sighted choices. Always weigh the present enjoyment of your pleasures against the necessary consequences of them.

It is more useful to be a great listener than to be a good speaker, if you learn how to follow up on what a person tells you during a dialogue. You can be regarded as an excellent conversationalist if you learn how to listen and follow up well, without ever having to be good at telling a story about yourself.

Be exceptionally wary of any individual who seeks to befriend you in a way that is very aggressive as they nearly always do not have your best interest at heart. This is especially true if they are someone you randomly meet, such as on the street, especially outside of a place such as a bank or train station.

You should seek the endorsement of others who can benefit your business efforts while simultaneously not allowing the endorsement of others' products or services to cloud your own ability to investigate and verify what you are being told. Celebrities and business leaders can make mistakes in their endorsements and fraudsters can take advantage of them, too. Be mindful of what you do, who you associate with and if something seems suspect or shady, it probably is.

It is worthwhile to know that it has become popular for people to make demands and have unrealistic expectations based on what happened during a past they never lived in nor experienced. As you study history you will see that much of recorded history involves constant warfare between nations who make and enter treaties with one another, only to later break the promises and war to begin again. Breaking contracts and promises were commonplace in past eras, which is why our modern civilization has developed a strong system of civil law to heavily punish oath breakers who fail to keep their end of an agreement. The people who fixate on trying to wrong every broken oath made by past generations by awarding reparations to the present generations are not focusing on building the new and present world; there is a never-ending amount of misfortune to be seen in the past and trying to 'rectify' it by rewarding people who never experienced any of this misfortune is a useless activity. Do not dwell yourself in such a direction, as it has no end. Instead focus on building the new.

Lastly, if someone promises to assist you with something but requires to learn some kind of secret information about you, your friends, your employer or your family and will this person will only provide you the assistance if you provide these secrets to them so that they can have something to blackmail you with to prevent you from betraying them, you should withdraw yourself completely from having any further contact with that person. Do not become subject to blackmail and indulge them, for once a person can successfully blackmail you then they can continue to hold that information over your head to continue to manipulate you.

On Maintaining Good Relations with Your Family

It is normal for children to bicker and gripe but as adults it is important to maintain unity, especially to ensure that the generational wealth and fortune of the family does not dissipate through poor choices.

It is necessary for you to spend holidays with your family, and this includes the extended family. It is a tragic thing that the breakup of the family has divided families, especially when we consider the consequences of divorces and remarriages. With such broken families it becomes impossible for the traditional communal feasting of Christmas, Thanksgiving and other kinds of holidays, which are festivals whose practices descend from other past holiday events. These events are more than just dates on a calendar; they are traditions designed to give families excuses to take a break from their own pursuits to come together and renew the bonds of family which are vital for the accumulation of generational wealth. Without shared holidays families fall apart and the bonds fade away. This is also why it is necessary for an ancestral home, because you need an estate for family to be able to gather at, and the larger your family the greater the need to provide boarding for family members to stay for the holiday while visiting. This is not something many people consider anymore because the breakup of families from divorces have largely eradicated tight family bonds that are renewed during the holidays but if you are to turn the tide back toward a more stable society, this familial tradition must be renewed in you. You cannot do this if your family is scattered and unable to gather at a family estate.

On Seeking Adventure

One of the necessary steps to become an ideal man is to have successfully completed at least one great adventure. As mentioned previously there are three kinds of great adventures, military service, exploration of unknown places and entrepreneurism. I have discussed the latter in a prior chapter on building wealth; here we will discuss the other two.

Military Service

When I was seventeen-years old I dropped out of high school, earned my General Education Development certification and enlisted into the US Army. I served five years of service and deployed during Operation Iraqi Freedom. I won't claim that my military career was anything extraordinarily or unique, as I do not believe it was. Yet, the experiences did shape me for the rest of my life

The epitome of masculinity is to be a soldier. I do not say this to glorify war. I say it because it is true. To be a soldier is to serve your community, your nation, and family legacy. It is something that requires all of the Virtues to do responsibly.

Men have always been expected to be willing to sacrifice their lives for the defense of their families and nations, and although women may enlist in our time, it will always be men who do the bulk of the fighting and therefore, the sacrificing of life and limb.

Military service is often the most direct way for a man to increase his social class in any society, through merit and achievement. Ideally, one should strive to become an officer but in the absence of a commission, enlisting in any rank is a noble thing to do.

If you are born into low social status as a man, joining the military is the most common means of improving social status. The military provides you job skills training, shelter, food, clothing and reliable pay. There are few careers that a man with limited resources can choose that provides as much as the military can. If you can achieve enough merit, your service can open doors for you when you are discharged, not only with the skills but also with the reputation you earn from the missions you accomplish. There will always be people who respect those who have served in the military, especially those who have had adventures as a soldier with tales worth telling.

There are plenty of advantages of joining the military. A lot of doors become open to you. While in the service, you will undoubtedly learn new skills that will serve you in the military and afterward. Countless people develop excellent habits, resulting in the top-notch physical condition and the confidence and talents required to succeed in life.

Furthermore, you'll find yourself able to take advantage of a seemingly endless list of programs, scholarships and the like. Many people use military scholarships to attend university before or after their services. With advanced degree programs which the military helps pay for, you can be set for a career after you've been discharged.

The advantages of joining the military also include benefitting from the sense of fraternity felt throughout all five branches. Networking and making friends for life can help ensure you have the contacts you need to excel in life.

There are of course some disadvantages to the life of a soldier as well. Discipline is taken extremely seriously in the military. If you cannot follow orders and adhere to the values and ideals of the military, you will find yourself unable to function optimally and might even get drummed out. This will lead to a dishonorable discharge, that will restrict your employment opportunities for the rest of your life. Many people will not trust someone who has flunked out of the military and you will not receive any benefits, nor be able to join fraternal groups for veterans.

There is also the possibility of injury and death. Injury is possible even outside of battlefields, as training exercises can still have a level of danger to them. Your freedom is also restricted and you will have little choice in assignments. You will however end up journeying to places you never expected to go, and places most Americans never see. Such is the life of a soldier.

My advice to young men who are thinking of military service when they come of age is to prepare years in advance. You must ensure you have hand-to-hand combat skills – the military will not spend a great deal of time training you for this, but they are useful. During recruit training, such as boot camps, some recruits may try to bully you and the only way to earn their respect is to be strong enough to not be pushed around. You of course also want these skills for if you need to fight in close quarters, too, as sometimes you may be ambushed and not ready with a weapon, or have a firearm jam on you. The vast majority of combat is done with firearms in this age, and the military will train you in these tactics, but if you wish to gain an edge then it can be useful to practice games such as paintball or airsoft to gain some experience with tactics. Having experience with being able to shoot will give you an advantage in earning marksman badges, which are necessary for promotion.

You should of course also be athletic and able-bodied if you desire to enter the military. When I was around thirteen years old, I decided I would enlist, and so I spent most of my time as a teenager studying martial arts and exercising to build up my body to prepare for military service. I also gained experience shooting rifles and handguns, too. Not every teenage boy has this opportunity in the current society we live in, as many boys are fatherless or live in families where parents do not have access to firearms, but even without this you can do your best by preparing your body and mind for military service.

Exploration of Unknown Places

Exploration of the unknown requires travel, which has a cost. You must be able to carry the cost of the trip yourself, which requires both planning and possessing necessary skills to earn money while you travel. Otherwise, you need to have obtained wealth to allow the travel in the first place.

Regardless of the situation you find yourself in, never randomly stop and consult a map or otherwise appear to be visibility lost. There are people who will take advantage of you, usually by mugging you or misleading you into an ambush. You should stop at a sheltered place such as a restaurant to find your bearings. Also, you should generally avoid stopping when someone randomly asks you something such as what time it is or some other thing, as they may be seeking to get you to stop so they can pull a knife or gun on you, or to simply grab your watch or phone and sprint away with it. On this note do not wear headphones in public unless you are at a gym, as you will not be able to hear if someone approaches you from behind if music is blaring in your ears.

On this note when you are in a fight, always flee after you win the battle. You will probably be arrested by the police if you stick around, regardless of who instigated the crime, as they will charge you with assault even if you were just defending yourself. The prosecutor may not fully charge you with the crime after a proper investigation, but police will often arrest you anyway, just in case a prosecutor decides they want to. So, flee the area if you can to avoid having to deal with this, especially if no one knows who you are.

On Heroism and Becoming Heroic

The label of hero has been diluted by corporate branding. We now award people the label of hero simply for being a celebrity who has accomplished something that many people admire, such as becoming a professional sports athlete or a successful movie actor. But these people are not genuine heroes, for to be a true hero requires life acted in the service of virtues, most specifically, in the service of those values which society deems necessary. You must live a virtue-based life if you wish to become a genuine hero.

You must be wary of selecting the wrong values to champion, as many people have done misguidedly. Although you may be applauded by others for championing a value they share, people can be mistaken if they do not apply an evidence-based approach to their lives. There are those who make decisions rooted in superstitions and fantasies, and feel that dedicating their lives in the service to these things will produce good results -- yet they often don't. During my lifetime many people dedicated themselves to the overturning of laws that prevented commercial sale of narcotics and when these laws were overturned, it greatly destabilized many communities as people indulged in them, becoming crazier and making poor choices in all facets of their life. This led to an epidemic of vagrancy in many cities, which led to increased crime. It has become the case that in many cities the bulk of emergency calls for police involved vagrant drug addicts who had vandalized, robbed or even killed people. This was the unfortunate result of many people deciding to value independent freedom to intoxicate themselves over valuing moderation and self-control of the worst of their instinctive impulses.

The difficulty for many people to identify a path of evidence-based virtue is why I spent so much of my life developing the philosophical framework of Chivalric Humanism. I wanted to guide people away from irrational approaches to navigating life, and to encourage them to instead follow the path of science, logic and excellence.

Simply having the correct values and feeling secure about it is not in itself heroism. True heroism is in taking action in the service to those values, regardless of however difficult it may be to do so. Indeed, the more difficult it is to take action in service of those virtues, the greater the hero you are for having taken this action. This is why those who have sacrificed their own lives for their values are considered to be the greatest of heroes and regarded as martyrs. Yet, I tell you that the greatest of heroes is not the one who will throw away their life carelessly for virtue alone, but one who is able to accomplish the goals in service to those values and in doing so, make the world a better place than it was when they came into it. Therefore, a life spent in service to values and virtue that serve mankind at a mass scale is a harder sacrifice to make than simply sacrificing your life in a moment for a single action. It is harder to devote the years of your life to the accomplishment of a goal of such importance and ideally, this is what you are better suited to focus your efforts on. Self-sacrifice of your life should be avoided if possible, as it prevents you from doing more good with your remaining hours. Besides this, the path of the hero is one of self-fulfillment of your values, and it is how this self-fulfillment benefits the lives of others is what makes a person a hero; it is not the sacrifice of your life for another on principle alone. Self-sacrifice can be heroic, but it is not a requirement of heroism.

To end this part I leave you with the follow words of Friedrich Nietzsche from *Thus Spoke Zarathustra*,

"It breaks my heart. Better than your words, your eye tells me all your peril.
You are not yet free, you still search for freedom. Your search has fatigued you and made you too wakeful.
You long for the open heights, your soul thirsts for the stars. But your bad instincts too thirst for freedom.
Your fierce dogs long for freedom; they bark for joy in their cellar when your spirit aspires to break open all prisons.
To me you are still a prisoner who imagines freedom: ah, such prisoners of the soul become clever, but also deceitful and base.
The free man of the spirit, too, must still purify himself. Much of the prison and rottenness still remain within him: his eye still has to become pure.

*Yes, I know your peril. But, by my love and hope I entreat
you: do not reject your love and hope!
You still feel yourself noble, and the others, too, who dislike
you and cast evil glances at you, still feel you are noble.
Learn that everyone finds the noble man an obstruction.
The good, too, find the noble man an obstruction: and even
when they call him a good man they do so in order to make
away with him.
The noble man wants to create new things and a new virtue.
The good man wants the old things and that the old things
shall be preserved.
But that is not the danger for the noble man — that he may
become a good man — but that he may become an impudent
one, a derider, a destroyer.
Alas, I have known noble men who lost their highest hope.
And henceforth they slandered all high hopes.
Henceforth they lived impudently in brief pleasures, and
they had hardly an aim beyond the day.
'Spirit is also sensual pleasure' — thus they spoke. Then the
wings of their spirit broke: now it creeps around and it
makes dirty what it feeds on.
Once they thought of becoming heroes: now they are sensu-
alists. The hero is to them an affliction and a terror.
But, by my love and hope I entreat you: do not reject the
hero in your soul!
Keep holy your highest hope!*

On Owning a Pet

Dogs tend to be associated with masculinity because dogs have historically served as companions for hunters and used as tools for other kinds of work, including for shepherding. These are all trades historically performed by men.

Dogs take after their owners. An unruly and disobedient dog is reflective of its owner's own lack of self-control. If you cannot tame a dog and train it well, you will not be able to do the same with a child, either. Owning a pet is preparation for how to raise a child because a pet is essentially a baby that will never grow up. How you treat your dog will be how you treat your son or daughter; overly spoiling a dog and it becoming disobedient, barking madly at everything and jumping all over people means you will raise a child that is equally without restraint and annoying to others, and likely stupid.

If you can raise a dog to be disciplined and learned, steadfast and loyal, and who understands their place in the social hierarchy then you may understand how to lead men, too. It is also applicable to becoming a father; if you cannot train a dog, you will not be able to train a child any better.

You should not own a dog unless you have ample space for the dog to run and roam. Dogs kept inside a small space like an apartment become bored and frustrated, and also tend to become confused and can be alarmed when in the outside world. These dogs become the most territorial of the

Women are largely associated with cats as a pet in modern culture because for hundreds of years cats were given as a present to a young bride on her wedding day, beginning with Scandinavian Viking peoples, and this cultural association with young girls and cats has remained. The primary purpose cats were domesticated is to catch pests such as rats and mice that will taint food supplies. A cat that does not serve this purpose and simply exists to lounge in your house is not able to fulfill its instincts; it will become bored and destructive of your property in its boredom, in addition to becoming incredibly needy of your constant attention to curb its boredom. This is something to remember.

Pets are a luxury. They are also a responsibility. There are times when a man can afford neither the luxury nor responsibility of a pet.

On Enduring Hardships

After I had earned my first million, I commissioned a painting of a family crest, of my own design. From the ancestral Martel family crest of three crowned golden hammers against a blue shield I simplified the design to a single golden crown hammer against a blue shield. As there are no ancestral family words I am aware of, I selected, '*Nobis eduro*', which is Latin for '*We Endure*'. This is something that my grandfather August Martell; would sometimes say in times of frustration, "*We will endure*" or "*The Martells will endure*". But it is also reflective of my life as a whole; throughout every hardship or struggle that has left me feeling distraught with grief so terrible I thought I would die of heartache, I have managed to endure it and find a way to thrive. I therefore impart these words to you about how to overcome hardships and hope they will comfort and guide you in your times of great need for guidance.

Through the course of all men's lives you will encounter hardships and struggle vigorously. These are the seasonings of the soup that makes a man flavorful. Much like how the steel used to forge a sword must be subjected to fire and pounded into shape, so too is the spirit of a man forged by the challenges he faces and the tolls his mind and body takes. The more disastrous the misfortune you can overcome the stronger your inner willpower will be. The strongest man is not the one who can knock down men easily with his fist in the boxing ring, but the man who can take the strongest blows and keep standing on his own two feet despite whatever his opponent throws at him, for this is a man whose strength extends outside the boxing arena. As such you must learn how to integrate the shadows of life into yourself and move forward still.

We sometimes have no control over all of the factors which affect our lives and the only thing we can truly control is how we choose to think about the actions of others and how we act back in kind. We can choose to be defeated by those that seek to rob us, or we can choose to fight back. We may lose in the effort, but we can at least choose whether or not we will be a victim or a fighter.

We also choose whether we will become weak willed men who turn to the bottle to lick our wounds. It is tempting to escape alcoholism or other psychedelic drugs to provide immediate distraction and excitement, especially when we feel miserable and frustrated due to hardships. But you must not give in to this temptation for it will reduce years of your life and greatly reduce the quality of the ones you have left. There are people who convince themselves it is totally fine to smoke marijuana because it is legal in many states but the reality is that marijuana growing frequently involves the usage of pesticides to maximize the harvest and the processing method of the leaves to produce the weed often leaves large amounts of the pesticides on the leaves, which people then smoke in addition to the other health side effects. Your efforts to be successful will be frustrated by your addictions should you develop any.

Throughout the course of your life you will experience betrayal. Betrayal is only possible because you trust another, and this betrayal will caution you against trusting again so quickly.

But I ask that you do not let such things color your interactions with all people and fault others who have done you no wrong. Still, you must learn to differentiate those worthy of trust from those who are not, because in the end, you trusted someone that you should not have and that is why you were betrayed. The more important a thing is, the more secretive you should be about it. There are some things in your life which you should never trust anyone with the knowledge of, not because no one could ever understand or be trusted with this knowledge but because the opportunity cost should you be betrayed is too great to risk anyone else possessing this information. Do not live your life believing that you must share everything you think and know with another person such as your wife or children, because there are some things best left known only to yourself.

As Mark Twain once said, '*Every man is a moon and has a dark side he shows no one.*'

Lastly, I advise you to be wary of those who upon meeting you and hearing of your ambitions are instantly ready to support you and be your friend; there are always people seeking to take advantage of the disadvantaged and heart broken. You do need allies in life, but always be cautious in your dealings with them. All business agreements must be enshrined into a properly drafted legal document developed with legal counsel that represents your interests. Always consider the prospect that an ally today could become a thief tomorrow. Sadly, it is rare these days to have genuine friendships with your business partners and while this is disappointing, it is necessary to remember. You should always be warm and friendly to others, and be charming but filter everything a person does through the understanding that their primary motivation of interacting with you is to obtain wealth for themselves. You are the only person who can truly look out for your own interests, and while a lawyer can guide you on this, you must make intelligent choices for yourself, too. Not every lawyer is a competent lawyer as well, which is why it is necessary for you to also have some knowledge of business laws even if you are not a lawyer yourself.

Raising Children

It is my opinion that many in the current generations of parents in the West have forgotten the important lessons of their ancestors when it comes to raising children. Many parents today have pregnancies accidentally instead of intentionally, and there is no actual plan for how they will raise their child, which they prepared for in advance. Even among those parents who intentionally have children they spend no time thinking deeply about the best way to raise their child; at the last minute they try to learn how to be parent, as if simply reading a few books is in itself a plan on how to raise a child throughout its years into a successful adult in their own right. This is different than past generations, where teenage years involved parents teaching boys how to become good fathers and girls how to become good mothers. This is rarely done anymore, as many parents don't know how to do it, either.

Many parents today believe the schools will educate their child in everything that is required of them to learn and because this is not the case, the child grows up to fend for itself; this rarely works out. The lack of preparation and guidance of the child by their parents only allows the most intelligent children with the best of personalities to succeed as adults.

Prominent families who acquire, maintain and grow generational wealth plan their families over the generations to ensure this stability and growth. If every child is expected to make his fortune with no assistance from his family it significantly reduces the prosperity for all, since children may spend years trying to acquire assets their parents already obtained and which the child ultimately will inherit anyway, but only after the death of their parents at a time when these assets may have less value or worse, when the child does not know how to best utilize these assets because they did not have any experience with managing that kind of wealth. Prominent families therefore teach their children how to manage wealth and use a small amount of the family estate and resources to grow new streams of wealth so that by the time the parents pass and inherit their assets good fiscal behaviors have already developed in the heirs. Wealthy individuals who fail to teach their heirs these lessons find their fortunes lost within a generation after they die, their descendants often coming into poverty and their bloodline potentially even ending completely. The biggest mistake that parents can do is believe it is not necessary for children to learn how the parents gained success by learning the same skills and behaviors that led to their parents' success, with the parent's believing they struggled so that their children would not have to and could live a better life. Yet without the lessons the child is unable to appreciate the status they were born into and cannot manage the affairs of the estate they are expected to inherit.

Unlike other animals which are born with natural talents to defend themselves within a few weeks of their birth, humans are born naked and defenseless; they rely heavily on their parents for protection for the first few years of life as they learn to acquire culture such as language and other valuable skills. Small children must be protected and raised correctly with proper guidance so that they will grow up and be able to make a positive contribution to society.

As men we pass on our genetic legacy and adaptations gained in our lifetime to our children, but our wisdom can also be passed on as well -- and should. Our wisdom can also be passed on to others outside our lineages, who can then pass this wisdom onto others as well. This is the duty of a gentleman who is a productive member of the human species.

How to Be a Good Father to Your Children

It takes a lot to be a good dad, and you can't take it for granted. When you become a parent it's important that you do what you can to make your kids feel loved and cherished, as well ensure they grow up to become stable, well-adjusted adults who can succeed in their own lives and ultimately become good parents, too. There is a lot of literature on what makes a good father, but I'm going to give you my thoughts on the qualities of a good father.

Being a good dad is not easy, but it is rewarding. It's important to be involved in your kids' lives and be a good example for them. The qualities of a good father are hard to measure, but they're essential to raising children. Here are some tips on how to be a great dad.

Be Committed to Your Family and Community

A good father is a man who is not only committed to his family but also to the larger community and society. Being a good father means being involved in the community, making it a priority in your life. The area that your kids grow up in will impact the development of their personality, as the local community culture contributes to a child's own identity. It is a good idea to not only pick a good community to raise your kids in, but to yourself be involved in the culture of that community and how it is shaped.

Treasure the times you spend with your child. The time will pass you by faster than you can imagine. If you don't start making more time for your child now, he or she'll still love you but resent you for it later. Whatever he or she likes to do, you do with them.

Do you enjoy playing computer games? You should do it with them.

Do you like going to the movies? You should do it with them.

Read a book together. What about painting, or drawing, or building something? Whatever they happen to like to do, you should do it with them. This shows that you care about them and what makes them happy, and it's a good way to form good memories from bonding together.

Be a Champion for Your Kids

A good dad is a person that is loved, appreciated, and remembered because they were always there for their kid when they really needed someone to be their champion. A good dad is one that never gives up even when things get tough, and he stands up for what he believes in until the end. He is one that is present in his children's lives for the good and bad times in life, and therefore is not easily forgotten. His kids view him as a role model and guide for how to live their own lives, and by being a role model his kids naturally wish to model themselves after his better qualities.

To be a good father, you also need to learn patience and how to be attentive in your children's lives. You can't just become easily frustrated and give into anger every time they disobey you. When you punish them, the punishments must be appropriate and fit the offense. Minor mistakes should not be heavily punished and major offenses should always be punished.

Being a champion sometimes means having the courage to allow your kids to make their own mistakes and being there for them when they fail. No one can know what they are capable of achieving until they try to do it, and failure is a normal part of life. It is important for your child to strive hard at things and still fail at them, because learning how to pick oneself up from frustration and despair, to still strive hard again to succeed, is an important quality for achieving success in life. No one can accomplish great things with success every single time; success is often the consequence of having never given up and continuing to try to do better the next time. Your child has to learn this for themselves and if you try to be too over-protective, to always do your child's homework for them or become angry at others when they fail, your child won't emotionally develop correctly and may become someone that is spoiled or unmotivated. They have to learn the value of failing and getting up again to keep trying as a child, as this is a difficult quality to learn as an adult.

Be Responsible and Take Ownership of Your Duty to Your Kids

To be a good father, you need to involve yourself in your child's life. You need to be committed to be a part of your child's life.

Raising a child is one of the most important and rewarding jobs in the world. A real man accepts this responsibility and stands beside his children through any storm that life throws their way. He doesn't pass the buck to other people, deferring judgement to so-called "experts" that claim absurd things are good for children. If you suspend your good judgment and allow child psychologists and teachers to become the parent, then you will raise problematic kids. The teachers and school counselors are only responsible for the kids for a grade year or two. You have to be responsible for the kids for their full 18 years of life as a minor, and often even beyond then. The future of your family line will depend on how successful your kids are as adults and it is your job as a father to prepare them to be a successful adult. The so-called experts are typically short-sighted, often only caring about how grade performances and behavior issues impact their own job performances. It is ideal for most teachers for kids to be passive and just sit in class passing tests with high grades, and they don't have any vested interest in your children actually growing up into a functioning adult that is healthy, mentally well-adjusted and can succeed in life. This must always be understood.

The best role model for children is a good father that is invested into their growth from babes to adults. You want them to be well rounded individuals; a child that receives good grades but is unathletic, who has trouble socially and making friends, and who has little drive or motivation or passions, is a child that will not grow up to be a stable, functioning adult in the real world. Again, it's important to have balance in life. With current school trends focusing only on academic performance and anything else deemed a distraction, it is your job as a father to ensure your kids participate in sports, learn how to make friends, stand up for themselves against bullies and explore fields of interest in after-school programs. It is your responsibility to help your child cultivate their talents; don't expect others to take on this responsibility for you because teachers usually will not. They have no long term vested interest in your children's lives.

Teach Your Children Good Qualities by Cultivating These Qualities Yourself

Being a good dad is one of the most important things you can do for your children. Being a good father to your kids means teaching them about the value of hard work, perseverance and integrity. These are certain qualities that you must have in yourself in order to be a good father. You also need to be a good listener who can guide his children and encourage them to succeed.

To be a good father, you need to be a good man first. This means being honest, being responsible and showing your children that you are committed to always doing the right thing. You should also be thoughtful, considering what will make them happy, especially during times when your child might be depressed or sad about something.

It is important that you are also fair and honest in all your relationships, especially with your children and the people that your children see you interact with. Your children will learn right from wrong based on how you behave in your own relationships. If you are the type of person that teaches your kids it is okay to deceive and lie by observing you doing so, then they will become the type of people that become deceivers and liars. Ensure you take full responsibility for your acts as a husband or parent. Never make excuses for what goes wrong in your household as a way to dismiss your guilt.

To be a good father, you need to be there for your children. When you let your children down by not being present when they need you, they learn how to let people down in their own lives. They will learn how to make excuses for their own bad conduct from the excuses that you make when you let them down and disappoint them yourself, and how you make excuses for when you disappoint others. It's better to admit when you make mistakes and show the kids how to make amends, than to refuse to admit when you are wrong out of pride.

You must also train your children in how to be a good marriage partner -- be it a wife or husband -- and in how to be a good parent. This is one of the things which is almost never taught anymore; many parents send their children out into the world with no education in how to be a good romantic partner nor in how to be a good parent. This is frequently because the parents do not know how to be either, as they divorced their partner and they failed to be good parents themselves. But this must be turned around if we are to improve society at large, as too many dysfunctional children are being raised today who are not equipped in how to produce another generation of functional adults, and so the divorce rates continue to increase.

Your infant child must be spoken to frequently in order for them to acquire language and this must begin even in infancy and continue on at least until they are capable of reading a book such as Moby Dick on their own. The mother should spend time reading books to the child, even if they have not yet learned to speak, and this must happen every day. Many children today are greatly behind in language acquisition because their mothers do not do this.

By age four children should begin learning to assist the mother and father with basic household chores with more specialized skills for their gender role to learn starting at age six or seven.

Both boys and girls must learn martial arts and self-defense with weapons, as children are at a distinct disadvantage against adults and have no chance of physically overpowering one while they are a child. This is of critical importance, because it is estimated that around 800,000 kids go missing in the USA every year on average, and many are never found, so the crime statistics for kidnapping do not accurately reflect the situation as crime statistics only indicate successful convictions for crimes -- kidnappers, murderers and rapists of children who are never caught never get convicted and so the crime statistics do not accurately reflect actual committed crimes, only known crimes with successful convictions. As the parent it is your job to protect your kids but as you cannot always be present it is critical for children to be capable of protecting themselves against other adults and even other children who wish to harm them. This is especially the case if your family has wealth, as the child may be targeted by others seeking to ransom the child but ransomers often kill the child to help cover their tracks. This is not a pleasant fact, but it is a true one. So, teach your children to recognize danger and protect themselves from those who would harm them. If they do not know how to do this, they are likely to be killed by someone in the future.

Daughters should be raised to avoid becoming taken advantage of and sons should be raised to be protective of their sisters from other men that would take advantage of her. It is especially important for daughters to be instructed well in how to identify all kinds of frauds and deceptions, especially those involving cults and multilevel marketing schemes as women are especially vulnerable to these types of schemes, especially ones that involve pseudo-scientific ideologies such as veganism. Believing in one impossible thing makes a person more susceptible to believing in other impossible things of similar irrationality, and so a person who adopts some irrational beliefs becomes evermore susceptible to new self-destructive belief systems.

As a mother it will be part of her duties to educate the children, so girls do need to possess education in all of the same subjects as the boys, but daughters especially need extra consideration in being taught how to avoid becoming deceived by people she may find attractive and charming. This is because unlike men, women are hypergamous by nature and this makes a woman more susceptible to these types of con men. Indeed, con men frequently recruit women to help them recruit other women into multi-level marketing pyramid schemes and cults, and this must be explained to them. This is not to be done in a way to suggest they are a victim waiting to be victimized; it should be done to educate them of potential dangers in life, how to recognize them and avoid them.

It is important to understand that women are not inherently more organic thinkers and lack structure and coherency, as is often claimed. The reality is that due to hormonal cycles of menstruation that revolve around their fluctuating estrogen levels, women often experience emotions and feelings more intensely than men do, and without proper guidance they may allow their feelings to run wild.

By contrast, men do not experience these kinds of mood swings normally (outside of neurological conditions such as bipolarism) but due to a higher amount of testosterone, men tend to be more aggressive than women are, as testosterone makes effort and competition feel good. So, just as with girls needing to learn how to curb the undesirable aspects of their instincts, men too must learn to civilize themselves against their own unbridled instincts, too.

To say it plainly, girls must be taught how to calm their emotions to behave more objectively, and boys must learn how to channel their ambition in ways that are logical and constructive. The solution is the same for both, and so both boys and girls need the same education in logic, but they need it for slightly different reasons that reflect their differing biochemistries, and this should be remembered. The motivations boys and girls have for being emotional are different, even if the cure is the same.

Advice for Naming Children

Names are personal identifiers and will stay with a child throughout their life, unless the name is so horrific they desire to change it as an adult. A good parent should name their child something that will give them something to aspire to, as well as which will provide them good image in how the child is perceived by others.

A poorly chosen name for a child will result in others possessing prejudice against the child, especially if the name seems nonsensical, and this will greatly hurt the child's prospects for employment when they seek to apply for jobs, grants or even have correspondence with other people. Parents must therefore not name their child the way they might name a pet; you are naming a child who is inheriting your spirit and the future of your family legacy. Respect your child when you name them.

In Western countries names are usually in the form of a Personal name, the middle name and the surname. This generally matches the structure of the Roman praenomen, nomen and cognomen. It is therefore common for children to be given names that are Roman or Greek in origin.

Branch families are sometimes identified by a common middle name, but this practice has become less common in modern times. Today, naming conventions for children have turned into a compromise between parents, such as with the father choosing the first name for the son but the mother being allowed to bestow the middle name, some-times granting her maiden surname for the middle name. But I recommend against this practice unless the maiden sur-name is something that will inspire the child later in their life.

I discourage parents from choosing their children's names haphazardly, just because the parent likes the name. Names are words that have meaning, and people attribute personality traits to names. It is possible a child may decide to conform to a stereotype surrounding a name and so if that is the case, ensure the name is associated with positive per-sonality qualities, such as a famous cultural hero. As an ex-ample, Martin Luther King, Jr. was named after Martin Lu-ther, a famous preacher and in turn Martin Luther King Jr. became a preacher himself.

Specific Advice for Raising Boys

Young toddlers should wrestle with their fathers, and this should continue throughout the youth of the child's life. Be-ginning at age four the father should spend more time with the boy separate from that of the mother, teaching him mas-culine things. This helps re-iterate the boy's identity as a man, separate from the female nature of his mother and sis-ters. He should be dressed as a boy in breeches or shorts and the wearing of frocks should be entirely discouraged; a ten-dency some mothers want to do instinctively to feminize the boy but which a father must be mindful about preventing.

Young boys should begin taking a role in assisting the father with family business by at least age nine. Labor that is within their means should be focused on with no expectation for high performance, but rather to acquaint the child with the work and business so they are comfortable within the environment. It is about familiarizing the child primarily. They should also silently observe the routines of business such as minor business meetings.

A boy must become hardened for the world ahead and so must learn martial arts, participate in camping and hiking, biking and other sportsman activities.

A young man is likely to begin to exercise the limits of his rebelliousness during the age of fifteen to twenty. A way to limit this is to raise him to prepare for military service, and keep him invested in activities such as sports.

Specific Advice for Raising Girls

One thing to consider is that unlike with men, very intense athletic workouts and training can interfere with menstruation cycles and proper puberty development of girls. The reason is not fully known but I hypothesize it is the body assuming that the girl is in a time of danger, such as possibly needing to escape from predators or fight rival groups and so it is not an ideal time for reproduction of children. Our bodies do not know if we live in a modern technological civilization and many of our body responses assume a primitive wilderness environment with small tribes. Women can be athletic but trying to keep up with boys can be detrimental to her proper healthy development and fertility.

There are some women who seem to believe that femininity is something that can be discovered within a girl, but this is not the truth. There is no such thing as inner wisdom; It does not exist. Womanhood, like manhood, is a rite of passage and its qualities must be taught. We know this for an absolute indisputable fact because of cases of feral children and similar kinds of child neglect. Without introduction of culture at a young age the children develop no better than beasts driven purely by instincts.

If young children are not exposed to culture they will often never inherit it. In fact, they will not ever acquire language development at all unless they learn this skill as a young child.

Femininity is cultural and so it must be taught because culture is not instinctive. Culture is part of the technology development of early humans and just as you cannot intuitively know how to start a fire and must be taught this skill, so too much everything else that is cultural be taught to be known. Young girls MUST learn femininity as children or they will not obtain it. This is a biological fact about how humans develop from birth, that you have to learn these social skills as a young child, or certain parts of your brain will just never activate to be able to acquire other similar skills in the future of your life.

Just the sparks of what is human culture took millions of years to develop organically, through thousands of generations. A single person cannot reproduce it within their lifetime. The fruits of millions of years of cultural progress must be learned.

You can argue activities associated with femininity are "external", as many feminists tend to do, but at the end of the day, what else is there in life but the external world we live in and must interact with?

Suggesting inner femininity can just be "discovered" in a vacuum of the self is useless because a person will only have what culture they have acquired up to this point in their life to latch onto.

Arguably one of the primary reasons so many kids today are having trouble with traditional femininity and masculinity is because so many parents sit their kids down in front of a TV to be the babysitter, and the kids are imprinting on whatever comes across the tube and leading to them struggling with normal gender roles later in life, especially when they have been born to a 2nd or 3rd generation of parent who themselves spent vast quantity of time watching TV instead of spending time acquiring the rites of passage to womanhood / manhood from their own parent, who was too busy watching TV themselves to bother to teach their child anything.

I will say that girls should, like boys, also learn martial arts for self-defense, although it is not necessary to stress that she seeks high athletic accomplishment, as this can have a negative impact on her development during puberty if she tries to be competitive with other boys of the same age.

Girls should be raised so that they will make a good wife for a gentleman. Although the current trend is for women to be raised to be 'strong independent women' who are independent of men, this has proven rather disastrous for many women of my generation as it leads them to become miserable by around their forties and fifties; primarily because they were so independent they could not make a marriage work with a quality man, and now that their youth has faded most men are disinterested in settling down with them. Most of these women end up single mothers who struggle to pay their bills while introducing a revolving door of poor quality suitors in and out of the child's life, which leads to major problems for the children as adults who grew up in an unstable household. While it is possible your daughter could grow up to become a brilliant scientist, it is unlikely. Most boys will not grow up to become a brilliant scientist, statesman and such, either, despite the best of efforts. A person must be realistic.

By age fifteen a girl should be capable of performing many of the household chores, able to cook, sew, clean and manage many domestic affairs. As with boys, she still requires several years of education to be able to fully acquire knowledge necessary to be considered a well-prepared adult but more personal responsibility and independence should now be able to be trusted to her, depending on personality.

An important aspect of femininity is the ability to serve as an ideal hostess for guests at the family home.

Advice for Selecting a Good Wife

The first and most important thing is genetic screening to ensure you and the prospective wife are a good genetic match for producing children that are healthy and will inherit any genetic advantages that you possess. For example, the ACTN3 gene has a special genotype such as CC genotype, which allows the production of a special protein that gives a 2 to 3% advantage in sprinting, powerlifting and other sports involving the usage of explosive strength and speed. While a small percentage advantage like that seems negligible at an elite level it is the difference between a gold medal and not ranking for bronze at all. Furthermore, both parents must have a copy of this genotype of the children will not inherit it fully and produce the special protein. There are many mutations like this to screen for your mate to have if you have them, and there are also mutations to screen against such as a predisposition for numerous types of cancers and neurological disorders that might be regressive in your prospective wife but when your genes are added to the mix, will result in a high probability for those diseases to manifest in your children.

Many men are confused by the behavior of women in relationships. While I talk more expressly about how to select a woman with good personality qualities for choosing as a wife in later sections of this book, here are some useful tips.

General Tips for Selecting a Wife

Women expect men to be leaders in the relationship. If you give a woman everything that she wants and asks for, she eventually feels you are the submissive one in the relationship. Women generally find this to be unattractive and she loses respect for her mate as a masculine man, losing attraction for him.

Don't self-deprecate yourself by apologizing for things that you have not done wrong just because she has become upset with you and you wish to settle the dispute by taking responsibility and acknowledging blame. While there are situations where it makes sense to apologize, your relationship must not rely on you constantly suggesting you are needy, emotionally unbalanced and most importantly, desire her constant approval. A man who needs sympathy and comfort from his woman is generally unattractive to a woman, as she expects you to be her husband and not her child. A woman seeks in a husband a provider and protector for herself and her children, not a child that she needs to provide and protect. To this end a woman will often tease or ridicule a man in an effort to test his position and you should not become flustered at this, instead you should tease her back. For example, if she claims that you have a small penis then you should say that works out well for her because she is probably so tight a small penis is all she can take because nobody else wants to fuck her.

On that note do not use demasculinizing or gender-neutral language. It is not masculine to refer to your girlfriend or wife as "my partner". This is something gay men do and the reason heterosexual people have started adopting "my partner" in reference to their romantic partner is because they don't want to offend homosexuals. Using politically correct terminology to refer to your romantic partner because you are scared of offending someone who is not in your relationship is not a masculine activity and most heterosexual women will lose attraction for you if you keep up these kinds of submissive behaviors in an effort to appease people who are not in your relationship. So you should always refer to your significant other as your girlfriend or your wife if you are married.

You must do your best to avoid predatory women. All women by their nature are hypergamous; they wish to enhance their social status through their relationships. This is in contrast to men who seek to increase their social status purely through their own achievements. While a modern-day woman will also seek to enhance her social status through her career and education, they remain hypergamous and seek men of similar or greater education and income levels to choose as mates. While this is normal and expected, you have to use a woman's hypergamous nature to your advantage. This typically means not choosing a woman who has higher education as a wife or who has the intentions to have a career instead of becoming a homemaker.

While this attitude may seem dated and chauvinistic, the divorce statistics demonstrate that women who are not homemakers are far more likely to divorce a man. They also, because they are not at home with the children, are more likely to serve their children junk food because the woman has less time to spend at home cooking. They also place the children into daycare to be raised by strangers, some of whom may harm the children. These are all consequences of the breakup of the traditional nuclear family in the modern Western world and the long-term effects of this behavior has been largely detrimental to the raising of stable children who can grow up, be productive members of society and in turn raise their own children to be like themselves.

A boy must learn to let go of the desire to seek the approval of women so as to satisfy his self-esteem. He must learn to let go of this boyish desire for motherly approval and desire to be taken care of by a woman, and instead become independent and strong, as an ideal man.

Therefore, it is in your best interest to marry a woman in her early 20s who has not obtained higher education and has no intentions of having a career. You should focus on settling down with a woman whose main ambition in life is to be a mother and raise a family with you, supporting you as caretaker of the home. A woman whose social identity is focused on this makes for a more suitable wife and mother of your children over a woman who does not view being a mother as truly the first thing in her life; many women claim their children come first but if that was the case they would not spend the bulk of their time doing things other than directly caring for the children and which reduces the quality of the time they spend with their children, such as in the case of women who have no time to cook food healthy food for their children and instead serve them frozen dinners loaded with fat and sugars to mask the low nutritional quality of the food. It is also worthwhile to note that the nutrition of the mother when pregnant impacts epigenetics -- the gene expression of the child. So, if she is accustomed to a poor diet then the child will suffer for all of its life with poor gene expression compared to what it could have potentially been able to have. This, too, is why you don't select a woman who adopts unhealthy diets such as vegetarianism and veganism.

Trying to reconstruct a failed relationship is often unproductive because although you may have love for a woman based on prior experience with her, if a woman has broken your trust such as through infidelity it is unlikely you will ever fully trust her again. A woman will also believe she can break the most sacred of promises she can make to you and you will still reward her with your resources as a provider, and so the real penalties for her infidelity are absent. If there is no penalty for breaking your trust then she will continue to break it.

Presently in mainstream western society it is commonplace for a man to have the mistaken idea that a wife should love him in the same vein as how a man's first relationship with a woman was; that which he had with his mother. A mother will typically love her son unconditionally for who he is and tolerate many failings, never abandoning her love for him. This is not true of other women, however; women only have the capacity to love their children unconditionally. Women usually love opportunistically, in a way that benefits them.

Humans are unique in that during the first few years of life, we are extremely dependent on our mothers to care for us. This is not the case for other animals, which usually gain a large amount of autonomy within a few months after their birth. Contrast this to humans where for several years a human child is very reliant upon the parents, especially the mother, to care for him especially as the mother provides food through her breast. This relationship that boys have with their mothers creates an instinctive dependency on a woman early in a man's life, which cements the bond a boy will have with his mother, but it is a mistake for a man to believe such a bond is re-creatable with another woman, especially if she is his lover. There is also occasionally an issue where a boy may base his personal identity on that of his mother during his toddler years and up, instead of separating his identity away from the mother to imitate his father. This is often a result of the absence of a father in the boy's life in any prominent way so as to encourage the boy to develop into a man. For girls it is fine if they model their own emerging identity on the mother, as the girl will then naturally develop an identity of womanhood, but a boy must spend additional effort to develop into a man if he is to become successful as an adult. This abandonment of the unity the boy had with his mother's social identity in his first two years of life requires the presence of a strong father figure the boy will desire to imitate, instead of continuing to imitate the mother as the model for his self-identity. This requires a man to be active in the raising of the boy to manhood and for the mother to encourage the boy to imitate the father, not herself, so that a separation from the feminine identity role occurs organically and naturally for the boy. This is primarily achieved by the father through rites of passages and other kinds of tests which are unique for boys, including the participation in sports and such, that help foster the identity of a man in a young boy. Boys, unlike girls, must be initiated into manhood with effort. Manhood is not guaranteed and must be obtained through achievement, and initiation requires another man who knows the rituals of manhood to train the boy.

When you are dating make sure you do not accidentally impregnate a woman. It is advisable that you do not trust her claims to be on birth control as a woman can go off birth control at any time and simply not tell you she has done so, out of a desire to entrap you in a committed relationship. This is unfortunately very common behavior among women, especially those in their mid thirties who are wishing to have children before she reaches menopause. When using condoms you should dispose of the condom in a way she cannot obtain it, such as flushing it down a toilet. There are some women who have indeed tried to become impregnated this way, despite condoms today usually lined with spermicide, and impregnating herself with sperm that may have been damaged and will result in her giving birth to defective children. Only have children with a woman whom you are married to and when the conditions are correct for bringing a child into the world, which is when you are in a place of financial stability and have a proper home for raising the child in a stable environment.

Choose a wife who can cook for her children. Good cooking is something a woman should learn from her mother over the course of a decade, it is a valuable skill necessary for the raising of healthy kids that will not suffer health problems in adulthood. While kids raised on junk food may look skinny, this skinny-ness is partly because of the energy kids burn while playing but can also be a consequence of malnutrition. Bad diets practiced in childhood when practiced as adults inevitably lead to obesity and health problems.

Your wife must understand the value of good nutrition and what is necessary for a young man to eat while he is developing his physique; a young man requires more protein than a young lady does to promote his muscular growth brought on by puberty triggering changes in his body that create an ideal time for muscular growth. Your wife must do her part to support your son in cultivating his body through providing him nutritious protein rich meals, even if this means preparing meals specifically for him, as well as teaching him how to prepare his own protein rich meals so he understands how to take care of himself as a bachelor.

232

You must avoid a wife who believes grocery stores and prepackaged foods can replace the value of a well-designed, home cooked meal. A wife must pull her weight in the home instead of serving junk food such as frozen dinners, fast food and breakfast cereals. These junk foods create childhood obesity problems and lead to malnourishment. Far too many children are being served reheated fish sticks and chicken nuggets for every meal purchased in bulk from the frozen food aisles of grocery stores; these fill the belly but have high concentrations of fat to enhance the taste of the low-quality meat used in the production of the food.

There are some who will look at this advice and view it as not pro-feminist, and they are correct. Postmodern feminism ideologies are the primary root cause for the breakup of traditional family units, and you cannot acquire generational wealth and protect it without generations of descendants organized in traditional family units. Divorce results in the loss of generational wealth, and this is why even men who become millionaires and billionaires during their own lifetimes often fail to transform their fortunes into generational wealth; as these men lose their fortunes to wives and experience numerous divorces, the assets they can pass on to each child divides further and further. The children end up raised in unnecessary drama between their parents, forced to pick sides in the family disputes, and the fortunes squandered on family law attorneys and other vultures. The divorced women have a strong tendency to spend their gains irresponsibly and so they pass few of the assets to their children.

You must choose a wife who will be content as a stay-at-home mother and who is disinterested in competing with you for income and fortune, and whose natural tendencies toward hypergamy will not lead her astray to developing attraction to co-workers or bosses who she may view have a higher social class because of their relationship in her field of industry.

You should not interpret my words as a desire to prevent women from pursuing education. Women are free to make their own choices as individuals. I am merely saying the ideal wife is one who has no interest in pursuing higher education and having a career. A person does not need to have a college degree in order to have education and be intelligent. There is absolutely nothing preventing a woman from, while she is home with the children, pursuing studies on her own as an autodidact. I myself do not possess a bachelor degree nor much desire to obtain one, because I am an autodidact who can learn anything I am interested in through the reading of books. As I have no interest or need to have a diploma in these subjects as they are not part of my profession, I did not pursue this as an education. Yet I was able to generate nearly two million dollars before I was forty years old despite being both a high school and college drop out. Education and higher education are different things, and a woman who is a stay-at-home mother and caretaker does not require a degree to be such. Higher education should only be pursued for a career in which such degrees are necessary and there is no other need. Men can be highly successful in life practicing a trade that does not require a degree and generate sufficient income for the household, while his wife serves as homemaker. This is more stable for the raising of children than the post-modern dual income structure that leads to the problems I have already mentioned that lead to unhealthy, emotionally unstable children that will struggle as adults

It should go without saying there is no reason to use violence to solve disputes with your wife. Your wife is your partner in the raising of children and you using violence against her will not lead to a stable environment for the children, in addition to causing needless harm to your wife.

The Qualities That a Gentleman Should Want in a Woman

For those who claim I am being too 'chauvinistic' and 'disrespectful' so that they can justify dismissing my criticism of these women you should read carefully what I say. There is great value in women and men listening to harsh criticism of a how a person presents themselves in their dating profile, because so many women (and even many men) have latched onto postmodern ideologies that cause them to become miserable for most of their lives, especially after they are post 40 and cannot attract the kind of people they once could. It is of critical important for young men and women to have realistic understanding of the dating market if they want to find the "love of their life", which is not a product of magic

or wishful thinking but a product of taking the correct necessary steps to attract a high quality mate into your life and
then keep them happy in the relationship so they do not seek
to replace you. This kind of value requires effort and if you
do not understand what these efforts are you will never find
the happiness you wish to obtain.

Youthfulness is the Most Important Quality Men Want in a Woman

Youthfulness is the most important quality men want in a
woman. While dating apps allow young women in their 20s
and early 30s to become overwhelmed with suitors without
having to even leave their house, the same is also true for
men: older men have access to younger, more beautiful
women without having to leave our homes as well.

Younger women tend to date and marry older men
because women predominantly are hypergamous; they are
seeking to enhance their social status through romantic relationships. By contrast men tend to enhance their social status
through their own achievements and to attract a younger
woman to marry and procreate with. This behavior is deeply
integrated into the human species; indeed, in evolutionary
psychology hypergamy among women is considered to be
an inherent sex difference as part of the process of natural
selection amongst humans (*Evolution of Human Mate
Choice*, David C. Geary, Jacob Vigil, and Jennifer Byrd-

Craven & *Attractive Women Want it All: Good Genes, Economic Investment, Parenting Proclivities, and Emotional Commitment, David M. Buss, Todd K. Shackelford)*. Likewise, men prefer women who are younger because as a woman ages her chance of producing healthy progeny dramatically decreases.

Now, women who are subscribers to the irrational ideologies of third wave feminism believe their value should not be based on whether or not they have children and they instead wish to be valued by society the same way that men are. The problem with this is that the way men are valued in society is reflective of men's biological role in the human species, which is specific to male biology. It is the role of men to provide genetic information to the progeny that is based on gene adaptations the male has obtained during his lifetime and inherited from his own parents. Women, generally speaking, do not pass on any gene mutations developed during their lifetimes to their offspring as women are born with their eggs, a product of their parents' DNA. Women pass on gene mutations from their father via their eggs. What mutations women do pass on acquired during their lifetime is that of their immune system, specifically the antibodies of the mother which is passed on to her children.

So, women pass on one part of a chromosome pair via their eggs, which is a combination of their mother and father's chromosomes. Men, on the other hand, pass on their chromosomes as well but as sperm is constantly produced throughout a man's lifetime, he has great probability of passing on any mutations of gene expression he has gained during his lifetime. This is part of the reason why women have a strong preference for very muscular men and men by contrast generally do not care about how muscular women are when selecting a mate; it is men who need to subject our bodies to stressful situations and environments to acquire beneficial mutations, and muscle size (historically speaking) is directly related to the 'trials by fire' a man has subjected his body to. Our ancient ancestors did not have weight gyms or steroids; a man could only become very muscular by being a successful hunter who was able to consume a great deal of meat and obtain that meat by hunting. This activity built a powerful male body, and so women instinctively view men with powerful bodies as possessing valuable mutations to pass on to their offspring, in addition to having the strength to protect them during pregnancy (which is a very vulnerable period for a woman, especially millennia ago before the invention of modern medicine).

All of this is inherent to human instincts amongst us today; it cannot be changed just because you wish it to be changed. Our instincts were honed through millennia of behavior between our ancestors; behavior that started long before recorded human history and the invention of civilization. With few exceptions the vast majority of women will be attracted to muscular men forever and for always, as our ancestors' behavior has dictated our instincts. Even lesbian women when seeking sperm donors overwhelmingly prefer tall, muscular and handsome looking men when choosing what type of donor they want. There is no way to change this behavior with any kind of ideology; it is what it is. This is ultimately why third wave feminism, intersexuality and other pseudo-scientific ideas are fundamentally flawed; they do not accurately reflect the realities of our species and how we operate at an instinctive level. Any world view that ignores human instinct, where it originated from and how it influences every human's decision making is a fundamentally impractical ideology that will only lead people to reject their own leanings (which creates dysphoria) and become dissatisfied with the direction of their lives in old age once regret sets in.

Therefore, in modern relationships, men are valued based on their ability as providers of resources (shelter, food) and their physical health as determined by their athletic ability. Women are instead primarily valued by their youth (which is tied to less chance of birth defects in their progeny due to having higher quality eggs) and their willingness to be cooperative in a relationship with the male, specifically in the areas of ensuring their bodies are a suitable environment for incubating a child and then rearing that child while the man labors for work to provide resources (food and shelter historically, but now also things like education to the children and vacations for the family) for the family unit. While women can participate in obtaining resources, these are secondary concerns to her primary biological duties in the relationship, which is to be a suitable host for incubating children and then taking care of those children.

This is also why women who are overweight are viewed as less desirable; being overweight is an unhealthy environment for incubating a child as it increases blood pressure (*American College of Obstetricians,* www.acog.org/womens-health/faqs/obesity-and-pregnancy)

239

and other unhealthy behaviors that go along with a sedentary lifestyle. The knowledge overweight women make unhealthy mothers is something instinctive to men as well and cannot be changed by ideology or perception — men will always be more attracted to healthier weight appropriate women than overweight women as this is ingrained into our biology. (Men will accept an overweight mate due to feelings of 'love' and such, but sometimes due to underlying psychological issues men will have a fetish for obese women that is ultimately very unhealthy and leads to feeder fetishes as seen on TV shows about extremely obese people. The vast majority of people do not have these kinds of psychological problems that lead to such unhealthy fetishes. It's not good for someone to be with you only because he has a sexual fetish for an unhealthy lifestyle.).

Men also instinctively understand that women will take care of a child as well as she takes care of herself; if a mother is obese, the children will be obese as well, and develop the health problems related to obesity, too. Therefore, high quality men generally shun overweight women as mates.

Women who view these realities as 'unfair' are rejecting truth. Their rejection only works until they hit the wall in their forties and fifties; women who fail to find a loving husband by this point are almost exclusively miserable, regardless of their political ideologies. They simply no longer gain men to come into their beds that they are attracted to and must 'settle' for low quality men they otherwise would never have considered, and whom they ultimately are not as attracted to. Their relationships are chaotic and stressful as they try to make a relationship with a low value man work, whom they are never truly happy with.

On this note, women should stop treating men as a fashion accessory to their wardrobe instead of as a partner in a relationship.

Due to a confusion of hypergamous behavior, many women view taller men as possessing higher social status. Many women justify their preference for tallness because "when I wear heels I want him to be taller". The problem of course is that if you restrict yourself only to men who meet this height requirement you are eliminating quality men from your dating pool that would make good husbands and fathers; considering that most women wish to land a partner who earns six figures despite less than 10% of Americans make six figures annually (Economic Policy Institute, *Nominal Wage Tracker*), you are trying to go after a sliver of a sliver. Even worse, if a woman happens to be tall and insists only on marrying a man of equal height, she significantly harms her chances of dating; for example, in the USA only less than 15% of men are 6 feet or more in height. The average man is deemed as 5'8, but this of course is an average created by contrasting the shortest and tallest men, and is therefore not a useful metric for your dating life.

Treating men as a fashion accessory is therefore counter-productive if a woman's goal is to marry well. If a woman finds a man who makes sufficient income to support a family and will be a good husband and father, only a foolish woman would pass him up for superficial qualities such as whether he is taller than her when she wears a fashion accessory that she doesn't wear every day and likely will cease wearing much at all after her 40s.

As previously mentioned, older men can obtain younger women as natural selection drives women toward hypergamous behavior, and the most desirable men (with the most resources and social status) tend to be in their 30s and 40s, especially when looking at single men with athletic bodies and no previous children or failed marriages. Men with suitable income for supporting a modern family, with athletic bodies and who are not yet divorced or have children from a prior relationship, tend to be in their 30s and 40s. By contrast women who are young and childless (which is primarily what these high value men are seeking) are women in their early 20s.

Cooperation is the Second Most Important Quality Men Want in a Woman

When women reject their biological role in the human species they significantly reduce the pool of men that will consider them suitable for a wife. Even if a man procreates with a woman out of wedlock that is rejecting her role as a wife, he has an instinctive tendency to abandon her as a mate in search of another. This is one of the main reasons why so many single mothers exist; they were okay with being somebody's mother, but due to confusion about their role stemming from post-modern feminist ideologies, they did not want to be somebody's wife. Therefore, they could not keep their man.

The reality is that women who do not control their biological impulses and allow their inherent hypergamous nature to run wild in their youth tend to become miserable in old age; they trade 20 years of attention during their twenties and thirties for 60 years of misery and regret once they are post-forty. They become unable to attract the caliber of men they once did, many women becoming what is referred to as an 'alpha widow'; constantly longing to attract alpha men in the top percentile of attractiveness as they once did in their younger years but unable to do so because men can simply login to Tinder and find a dozen women younger and prettier than she is. Because she did not become a cooperative wife and rear healthy happy children for one of these 'alphas', he did not stay with her and moved on to another relationship because he was not emotionally invested in her to the degree he decided to be loyal only unto her.

Some women will dismiss what I am saying as "victim blaming" as they view themselves as victims of attractive men who have babies with them and then abandon them, but consider this; why is it that so many of your female ancestors were able to successfully keep their husbands and so many women today cannot? The answer is simply that third wave feminism and other postmodern ideas are counter-productive ideologies that make women uncooperative in the relationships and lead to them becoming abandoned. Or worse, it causes them to abandon men that make good mates to them because they are constantly chasing another man they think is more attractive or of higher social value, until they reach their 40s and suddenly discover they can no longer get those men to even consider a serious relationship with her anymore.

Cooperation is the most important quality for a woman after youthfulness. If you are not cooperative in the relationship with a man, a man will eventually abandon you. This is the biological reality of the human species as determined by natural selection and it is not going to change. Many women with boyfriends or husbands who repeat the same tired feminist talking points while in a relationship with her do not understand that once her youth is gone and her looks fade, the man will become less tolerant of her lack of cooperation in the relationship and if he can, will replace her with a younger version of herself even if the man has no interest in having more children, simply because this is how his instincts are driving him to behave.

There are younger women just a few clicks away. Until women accept the dating market is not actually in their favor — there are FAR more beautiful women in the dating pool than high quality men that make good husbands and fathers. In fact, high quality men are not restricted to women in their local geographic areas as we can also date women hundreds or even thousands of miles away from us (since we can travel to them or have them travel to us). Many high quality American men are actually choosing foreign women as wives because many Western women have adopted radical ideologies that make them unsuitable for wives and mothers of their progeny.

Women who wish to marry and be happy in that marriage *must* use their youth to land a husband that will be faithful and committed to her, and form a strong bond of loyalty through the mutual act of raising a family. If women fail to do this they will inevitably become an 'old maid' longing for someone to come into their lives that will "just appreciate them" for who they are, never realizing men do not appreciate women for who they are; men appreciate women for what they provide to their lives. And simply being "cute" is not enough; there are thousands of women in a 100 mile radius around him who are 'cute'. Most of them are not cooperative in a relationship with him, and that therein is the difference in what causes the relationships with him to work and others to fail.

If a woman does not signal she will make a good wife and mother to his kids, the vast majority of men will have no interest in her as anything but a playful tryst and a person to be replaced when a new woman who offers better value comes along. This means even women who get married, but don't have children with their man, are at a high risk of divorce because eventually the man will trade her in for a younger model if she becomes too much of a hassle for him to deal with in the relationship due to her lack of cooperation to his needs.

Many people need to stop confusing hobbies with what makes for an important relationship. Hobbies are fun things to do in your free time. No man of any quality will marry a woman because she likes the same TV shows and sports he does; he will only choose a woman and continue to be faithful to a woman because she adds value to his life with her role as a mother to his progeny and a cooperative wife in the relationship to him.

Sanity is the Third Most Important Quality a Man Wants in a Woman

Sanity can also be considered 'the least amount of baggage'. Basically, if you cover yourself from head to toe in tattoos, weird piercings and other body modifications, dye your hair weird unnatural colors that do not compliment your feminine charms then you are signaling to men that you have serious psychological problems and are greatly confused on what men find to be attractive. Likewise, if you have weird beliefs, such as believing in astrology, manifesting and other kinds of irrational nonsense, you will chase off high quality men who cannot trust you to make good decisions in the relationship. You will primarily only attract low quality men who don't believe they can attract or deserve a better woman, and whose own psychological issues will eventually cause the collapse of the relationship, too.

There are of course some men who are attracted to women who look like criminals. These are almost exclusively low value men with their own share of psychological issues, many of whom are abusive. They generally are not the caliber of men women wish to date if they think about the subject logically, and with the exception of some famous celebrities (celebrities are the exception because their value is based on luck more than anything; not every man, regardless of how attractive or his work ethic, can become a famous actor or musician, due to the nepotistic nature of the entertainment industry. A lot of celebrities are crazy drug addicts with severe mental illness, and whose success depends on their ability to lie well — which is ultimately what acting is), you will not find many men making six figures who want to marry women who look like a member of the Yakuza.

The rule of thumb has always been that a woman will take care of her children as well as she takes care of herself. So, if a mother looks like some kind of monster from a *Resident Evil* game, she will probably raise the man's children to look like that, too. Men who might have a fetish for women with tattoos and piercings generally do not want their own daughters to have tattoos and piercings, because they know how men such as themselves treat those women. One of the worst things a woman can do is confuse the attention she gains from low value men who will not make good loyal husbands and fathers with 'success'. It will all fade in her 40s and 50s and she will be left with a scarred body that attracts only dirtbags into her life.

The biggest problem with tattoos is that art is incredibly subjective; by covering your arms and chests with tattoos you significantly reduce the pool of men that will agree your artwork is attractive. You are restricting yourself to now only being able to marry a man who likes that type of art, which is a very narrow pool of men as art trends are constantly changing. Even more, most high-quality men are men like myself who do not have any tattoos whatsoever and have no desire to marry a woman who has tattoos. Most people with tattoos are gaining them for superficial reasons, and often to mark some type of trauma in their life they struggle to deal with. Having a constant reminder of your trauma you literally wear as a badge on your body is not a symbol of a person who is dealing with that trauma in a healthy way. You mark yourself to many people as a low value person when you mark your body with tattoos.

Women should also understand that due to interference from the political agendas of various groups, in particular third and fourth wave feminist activists, the therapy industry has been hijacked by many women who have severe psychological problems and cannot attract the kinds of men they want to date and marry, either. If your therapist is a believer in third wave feminism you should run for the hills, because they will lead you to be as miserable as they themselves have become.

A man must be able to trust and count on a woman to continue to be cooperative in the relationship. If she is not sane then she cannot be trusted to remain cooperative, and he will look to replace her — especially as women who are not sane are frequently a danger to himself, the children and others.

Instead of covering your body with tattoos and piercings in an effort to create a façade of being 'strong', it is better to deal with any underlying psychological trauma and learn to move past it in a healthy and productive way. If you make your personal identity your status as a 'trauma survivor' or a 'victim', then you will fall into psychosis and behave in ways that are counter-productive to attracting the type of man you wish to have in life. Many of your female ancestors lived in a harsh wilderness environment with predators, parasites and constant warring tribes. Losing a child was commonplace, and even rape occurred more frequently than it should.

Our female ancestors were subject to far more terrifying situations than the majority of modern women have ever experienced; they had to overcome this trauma and still find a quality man to settle down with and raise a family with, to pass on accumulated wealth and lessons to the next generation so they could make stable societies. You must learn to do the same and move past your own trauma to focus on what is actually important. This is the reality of life. You do not always get to decide what happens to you but you do get to decide how you choose to respond to it.

Lastly keep in mind that being too promiscuous is a highly negative quality for a woman. Regardless of the 'girl power' marketing that has become popular at present the chances of acquiring an STD greatly increase if a woman is very promiscuous. The number of women on dating sites with STDs is alarming, and promiscuous men are sleeping with these women and passing the diseases onto other women, too. In addition to this, women who are too promiscuous often find it difficult to emotionally bond to a man in a committed relationship and be content in that relationship, especially as she ages and her mate ages. Some 'alpha widows' are always comparing their present man to a previous man, wishing for the intense sex they once had earlier in life during their party girl phases, and it makes them frustrated in their marriages if their partner is not able to perform like a younger man as he ages. This is a toxic mindset that will only lead to a woman becoming extremely disappointed as few high-quality men tolerate so-called 'open relationships', which is just a way for a woman to cheat on her man to obtain the sex he cannot provide her while he continues to otherwise perform the duties of a provider. Eventually a man grows some balls and dumps a woman like this and moves on to another woman who will be more content with him; ideally one who has not had a wild party girl phase where she slept with numerous men she will also constantly compare him to during their new relationship. For these reasons being promiscuous is largely negative for the long-term happiness of a woman and will chase away high-quality men.

I hope this essay has been enlightening and is useful for women and men seeking to have a high-quality life filled with adventure, excitement and most importantly, genuine love and loyalty from a mate because they have transformed themselves into a person that adds genuine value to the relationship. The majority of women do not, and that is why they are on these dating apps for 40+ years and never finding happiness.

What is the Traditional Wives Movement?

The Tradwife movement is shorthand for the 'Traditional Wife Movement', a community of Western women who are rejecting many of the postmodernist feminist ideologies that have resulted in the rise of dual income households and consequent problems in society that have arisen as a result. In particular the tradwifers promote a lifestyle where the wife stays at home as caretaker for the children and household while the husband is the primary breadwinner of the family.

Over the past several years there has been a trend of interest in traditional family structures and rejection of post-modernism ideals of alternative family structures — in particular, a rejection of the third wave feminism that has gripped many Western countries, in particular the United States.

For example, by looking at Google Trends data we can see the term tradwife has seen a sharp increase in interest based on search queries for the phrase, and we can see which states have the largest number of populations interested in this topic.

Unfortunately, when you search for the term 'tradwife' on search engines like Google, you are often greeted by articles that are written by junk tabloid writers who treat third wave feminism as a religion. These radical feminists (who advocate for alternative lifestyles) dismiss the so-called "tradwife community" as being a group of racists or religious zealots. While I do agree the tradwife movement in the USA does appear to be rooted in conservative Christian communities, I have seen no evidence to suggest it has anything specifically to do with white supremacy. In fact I have observed black women talking about being "tradwives" — which should surprise absolutely nobody given that the vast majority of women around the world today and throughout all of human history, are essentially "tradwives".

While the "tradwife" movement has been mocked in the very liberal Western media, the reality is that the lifestyle Western tradwifers advocate for has been the norm for most of human history and it STILL is the norm in many non-Western countries, particularly those in Latin America, Asia and Africa. So to suggest its ideas are some construct of "white supremacism" is not only disingenuous, but ridiculous.

Men as the breadwinners and women as caretakers of the children is the norm in most of the world. It's only in Western first world countries that you see anything different, and this is a result of the embracement of feminist ideologies by these countries.

Why Has Interest in Tradwives Increased in the West?

It doesn't surprise me that more people in the West are becoming interested in traditional family structures, gender roles and marriages. Even as an atheist myself I can see that there are many advantages to a more traditional marriage structure and numerous disadvantages to the "alternative" lifestyle arrangements that many people are advocating which are completely experimental and have not been demonstrated to give children any advantages — in fact, as the studies I will cite in this article show, they greatly reduce a child's chances of succeeding in life and can expose them to abuse they would otherwise not be at risk for.

At the time I write this article, over 60% of children raised in the US attend daycare (*Encyclopedia of Mental Health*. 2016; 202-207, *Nonparental Daycare: What The Research Tells Us*, Noam Shpancer), and in my opinion, it shows how in these kids develop problems that were almost unheard of in prior generations. Significant social problems such as illicit drug addiction, homelessness, depression and mental disorders have increased in society as employment among women has increased. In the 1950s, only 10% of women with children had employment and drug usage aside from tobacco and alcohol was almost non-existent in the United States; this sharply changed during the 1960s and coincides with an increase of women's participation in the workforce to 38% (*Monthly Labor Review*, May 2002, *A century of change; the U.S. labor force, 1950-2050*, Mitra Toossi).

Now, I am not suggesting that women being able to have a career automatically equals high drug usage in her children. What I am saying is that the rise of mothers who work and do not stay home with their kids has dramatically increased the number of children raised in unstable environments and causes them to develop psychological issues that lead them to be more likely to abuse drugs. I am not alone in this belief, and there are numerous studies that demonstrate the negative consequences of children who are not raised in stable traditional households.

Studies Prove the Negative Consequences of Non-Traditional Households' Effects on Cognition and Behavior in Children

As of 2020, the United States has the highest percentage of single parent households of any country on the planet. 23% of children live in single parent households, overwhelmingly single mother households. By comparison Canada is 15%, but other countries such as China and India are just 3% to 5%.

US Census data shows that during the 1960-2016 period, the percentage of children living with only their mother nearly tripled from 8 to 23 percent and the percentage of children living with only their father increased from 1 to 4 percent. The percentage of children not living with any parent increased slightly from 3 to 4 percent.

Many studies have proven that kids raised in these environments, what is subtlety called a 'transitional household' (that is, where the parents are separated and constantly bringing new romantic partners into the kids' lives), do far worse in life.

Some examples,

- The research paper *School adjustment in sixth graders: parenting transitions, family climate, and peer norm effects* by L A Kurdek 1, M A Fine, and R J Sinclair serves an important example. It found that children who experienced at least one transition in family structure during early childhood were more likely to have elevated levels of behavior problems by age five, regardless of mother's marital status at the time of the children's birth.

- The study *Impact of family type and family quality on child behavior problems: a longitudinal study* by J M Najman, B C Behrens, M Andersen, W Bor, M O'Callaghan, G M Williams found that elementary school children who experienced two or more transitions were more likely to show disruptive behavior at school, to have poorer emotional adjustment, and to have lower grades and achievement scores compared to children who experienced no transitions or one transition.

- The study *Father Absence and Youth Incarceration* by Cynthia C. Harper and Sara S. McLanahan found that boys raised in a single-parent household were more than twice as likely to be incarcerated, compared with boys raised in an intact, married home, even after controlling for differences in parental income, education, race, and ethnicity.

- The study *Does Father Absence Place Daughters at Special Risk for Early Sexual Activity and Teenage Pregnancy?* by Bruce J. Ellis, John E. Bates, Kenneth A. Dodge, David M. Fergusson, L. John Horwood, Gregory S. Pettit, and Lianne Woodward, found that 33% girls raised by single mothers whose fathers left the home before they turned 6 ended up pregnant as teenagers, compared with just 5 percent of girls whose fathers stayed in the household.

Studies also show that children in daycare do worse than children that instead stay at home with a parent.

- *The Rise in Cortisol in Family Day Care: Associations With Aspects of Care Quality, Child Behavior, and Child Sex*, a study from the National Institute of Child Health and Human Development and the Institute of Child Development of the University of Minnesota, found that children who spend a large amount of their day in daycare experienced higher stress levels and aggression as opposed to those who stayed home. This was assessed through measurement of the presence of cortisol in the children's saliva.

This should surprise no one; daycare centers have extremely low standards to operate. All that is required to open a daycare center as a business is for the staff to be certified in first aid and CPR, and then submit an application for a business license. No special education credentials are required to open a daycare and there are no special programs required for attendance to provide training for daycare center workers by any state in the USA. This is probably why the majority of daycare centers are ran by people that have limited education backgrounds and operate them out of their homes, often letting the kids run around in their backyards and watch PBS television programs to occupy their time. The daycare owners have no long term vested interest in the developmental welfare of the children, as their client is only the parent and daycare centers have an abundance of clients due to so many women choosing to be working moms today. On top of this, daycare centers can receive money from states using HUD and welfare voucher programs meant for low income families to pay for their child care. This is exploited for fraud sometimes; one notable case involved (KC Daycare) defrauded taxpayers in the state of Missouri as much as $556,000 when the daycare owner exploited the state's Child Care and Development Fund. The case is also notable in that the daycare center had failed numerous inspections as far back as 2013, and yet was still operating until 2019 — the owner was even able to start new daycare centers even with his first one having failed inspections.

The kids are often more than just neglected in daycare though; a 2017 report from the U.S. Department of Health and Services on Child Maltreatment found that 2,237 daycare providers were found to be abusing and neglecting children in their care. On top of this, despite common misconception that child molestation is primarily done within families, a 2012 Department of Justice study titled Characteristics of crimes against juveniles found that 70% of children who are sexually abused are molested by an adult the family trusts.

Like, you know, a daycare center worker. In fact, if you were to do a search on Google Search for 'daycare worker abuse' you'll find a seemingly unlimited amount of articles discussing convictions and arrests, complete with even security footage of daycare workers abusing children. As an example that is sadly common among these cases, in 2014 a female daycare worker helped her registered sex offender boyfriend molest several children at ABC Kidz Child

Care in Elyria, Ohio, and she even participated in the creation of child pornography videos. Daycare centers are exploited by sexual predators to gain access to children, and there are cases where child porn rings have operated daycare centers for this explicit purpose.

Yet even though daycares are associated with development problems in children and place them at greater risk of abuse, US Census Data (2016 Current Population Survey Annual Social and Economic Supplement) shows that 62% of children have a mother who works outside the home. Since less than 5% of single parent households are stay at home dads, this means over half of the population of children who are raised today are being exposed to daycare centers that dramatically increase the chances of the kids becoming developmentally scarred — all of this as a consequence of radical feminists advocating for family and social structures that allow a woman to be "equal to a man" in the workforce but that also requires strangers (who may abuse them) to take care of their kids for them.

Currently the mainstream media is so fixated on gender equality in the workforce that we're ignoring the drawbacks to children who are not being raised by a stay-at-home parent, and then inevitably do grow up and become the adults who cause more problems in society as a consequence of what happened to them as a child. Per numerous studies on the subject, such as this one (*British Journal of Psychiatry*, December 2001, *Cycle of child sexual abuse: links between being a victim and becoming a perpetrator*, M Glasser, I Kolvin, D Campbell, A Glasser, I Leitch, S Farrelly) children who have been sexually abused are extremely likely to become abusers themselves, perpetuating the cycle and ultimately increasing the number of abused children each subsequent generation after.

Studies Show That Having a Stay-at-Home Parent is a Huge Advantage for a Child's Development — and a Significant Drawback if They Don't

Unfortunately, if you search for "stay at home mom studies" you get blasted with junk science polls from Pew and other garbage tabloids about if being a stay-at-home mom is "mentally healthy" and the economic status of stay-at-home mothers, and other nonsense that is designed to make it seem like stay at home moms are women who failed at succeeding in the workplace.

What Google hides in the search results are the studies that show the positive impact on children who are raised by a stay-at-home mom.

One prominent study in particular is actively buried in the Google Search results and which I want to emphasize here in my essay.

Published in the *Journal of Labor Economics* in 2014, *Home with Mom: The Effects of Stay-at-Home Parents on Children's Long-Run Educational Outcomes* by Eric Bettinger, Torbjørn Hægeland and Mari Rege studied the academic performance of 68,000 kids in Norway and found that children aged six to nine with a stay-at-home mom performed academically better in their test scores compared to kids that attended daycare.

259

The study is particularly good because Norway has a program called Cash for Care that provides a financial incentive for moms to stay home with the kids by providing financial aid to married couples who chose to have the female stay at home to care for the children. This means the study cannot be dismissed by claiming that it was only very wealthy families which saw these advantages; the study controlled for economic status due to the Cash for Care program allowing low-income families to have one parent stay home with the children.

This study should be the #1 result for "stay at home mom studies" and yet it is not. Instead, Google Search is suggesting junk science articles. I doubt this is an accident and I suspect it has been the consequence of a politically motivated engineering of the search query results to advance a political agenda by the Google employees who have access to the manual review tool for Google Search.

Regardless, the point still stands; the evidence that traditional family structure lifestyle has a very positive impact on children is undeniable. It is socially irresponsible for tabloid magazine writers to encourage women to be single mothers in light of this evidence and it is leading to more instability in society as larger populations of people are raised in unstable households.

Is the Tradwife Movement a Good Thing?

I think it is, although ideally I believe it would be more effective if the religious undertones were not focused on so heavily by those in the community. I think trying to push conservative Christian religious beliefs is not going to be very effective at convincing enough women to abandon third wave feminism for the culture to shift, as religious participation is definitely in decline and not likely to rise. Humans as a species simply know too much about our universe now and it is difficult to continue to believe in metaphysical viewpoints and still claim to be a person who makes intelligent, reasonable decisions in their life. It would also be better to emphasize how the mother tends to make more sense to be the one to stay home with the children given that men tend to select occupations that earn more.

The tradwife movement would do better to focus on highlighting the numerous studies that show that alternative lifestyle households harm the development of children and consequently create many psychological problems the child didn't need to develop and must now overcome in order to find success in life, as compared to his age peers who were raised in a more traditional family unit with a stay at home parent. This would be more successful at convincing women to participate in the community and give radical feminists less ammo to use to attack the movement.

I also think that feminism at its root, is quite fine and acceptable for a stable democracy to function. Democracies depend on perceived fairness of the system by its citizens in order to run well. It is difficult to have a perception of fairness if women don't have the right to make their own choices or have their opportunities legally restrained based on their genders.

However just because something is legal does not necessarily mean you ought to do it — seeing the long term social consequences over the past fifty years of feminism becoming ever more radical and antagonistic toward men has led to the creation of apps like Just a Baby that intentionally encourage women to become single mothers and consequently will doom those kids to be raised in an unstable household. Through misinformation created by radical feminists to advance their zealous political crusades , many young Millennial women are making the poor choice to intentionally have kids outside of marriage, with men who make poor fathers and consequently become single mothers. Worse still, some of these radical feminist ideas encourage women to divorce men simply for being bored in the relationship. Irresponsible writers and bloggers encourage women to intentionally make choices that will absolutely result in creating unnecessary obstacles between the woman accomplishing her goal of becoming happy, and tend to lead to misery. So an emerging community of women who are pushing back against this garbage is a good change, and I think necessary.

That does not necessarily mean that becoming a "tradwife" is a guarantee of success. I think women still need to pick good husbands and men need to be proactive in being good fathers. There is just as much bad information being spread encouraging men to "go their own way" that will inevitably lead to men being miserable later in life, too.

Still, I think more women recognizing they need to cultivate the qualities of a good wife and mother — the qualities I refer to as the Cinderella qualities in the next essay— is a positive thing for Western societies. It is better in the long term for society as a whole if children are raised with the most advantages possible and the least opportunities for developing psychological scarring that will haunt them for their lifetimes.

We need the children of tomorrow to fix the problems created by misguided generations over the past fifty years. The children cannot do that if the same poor parental choices that created the dysfunctional people who are causing the problems of today keep being made by new generations of parents. The bleeding can only stop when the experimental "alternative family lifestyles" of third wave feminists are abandoned and a voluntary return is made to more traditional family structures to raise new generations of kids that will become adults able to fix the problems.

If the bleeding continues, eventually there won't be enough functional and productive members of society in America to keep the machine of the economy running. The USA will then cease to be a super power, and the entire world will consequently become a much darker place as Communist Totalitarian countries like China supplant our country's role in global affairs, forcing its social credit system on everybody as a form of neo-slavery.

Perhaps you are okay with the real world becoming an Orwellian dystopian nightmare, but I am not.

So ignore the radical feminists who want to undermine the fabric of society by continuing to repeat the same mistakes over and over again. The Millennial Gentleman supports a return to more traditional family values and structures in the hopes of producing a better, more stable society.

Date a Cinderella, not a Tinderella

The majority of dating advice for men these days you will find on search engines are articles written by women who often have a vested interest in convincing men that women just like themselves make the best wives. If you're looking for a more objective viewpoint written by a man with a great deal of dating experience then this is the guide for you on what qualities you want in a woman to date and eventually marry.

While one might assume the obvious companion to a millennial gentleman is a millennial lady, the definition of what is a 'lady' is so broad today as to be rather useless. There are many women who call themselves ladies and use very loose definitions written by other women as the justification for these self-appointed labels. I personally would disagree that many of these self-described 'ladies' meet my own standards to warrant the term, but instead of having that argument I decided instead to come up with another label that can be more narrow to what kind of woman I believe makes the perfect partner to a gentleman these days.

The label I have devised is the Cinderella, named for the heroine of the famous fairy tale story. Of all the women depicted in these stories *Cinderella* is probably one of the few I believe who truly was deserving of the life she was rewarded with. Most of the others, such as *Sleeping Beauty* or the *Little Mermaid*, basically just sort of fell into happiness because they were just so gosh darn pretty that a successful high-quality man whisked them away. Cinderella, on the other hand, was a hard-working girl born into misfortune

264

who did her best regardless of the situation, always acting with grace to overcome adversities thrust upon her. She won the heart of the prince with her class that outshone all the other supposedly noble debutantes that chased him. This is the kind of woman that a gentleman should seek out.

Sadly, the vast majority of women who call themselves ladies and style themselves as divas, queens or princesses, are anything but. What the majority of these types of women are is what I call a Tinderella.

Tinderella qualities

A Tinderella is basically the kind of girl who has a personality type such as what the evil step sisters in the *Cinderella* story have. The Tinderella is the very definition of a narcissistic woman. They are selfish, cruel, fixated on superficial qualities and cannot handle any difficult situation. She is incapable of handling anything not going her way and will throw a tantrum if others do not give in to her. The Tinderella makes for a poor life partner, often creating unnecessary drama in order to make herself the center of attention. They believe they deserve loyalty from others but have none to offer in return. They are branch swingers who engage in hypergamy, always trying to find a better man whenever a relationship matures to the point that the man expects the woman to be loyal to him, which is far more commitment than the Tinderella is willing to give back. Inevitably she will vanish from your life as quickly as she entered it once she feels she has found a better opportunity for her short-term goals.

The Tinderella is often constantly on her phone texting away at her friends, even while on a date with you. She may even actually be on Tinder swiping away while you are treating her out to dinner. She may be sweet at first to convince you to treat her well, but she soon becomes a bitch to you. She treats you with disdain after she believes she has found a "better guy" and views you now as an obstacle to her short-sighted desires instead of a partner to build a happy life with. She may cause drama solely to encourage you to be the one to break things off with her, so that she can rationalize her disloyalty to you with the belief that you didn't love her enough to handle her at her worst so you "don't deserve her at her best"; never-minding that cute declaration didn't bring happiness to Marilyn Monroe and it won't bring any for the Tinderella, either.

(As a side note, while Marilyn Monroe was very beautiful and successful in her career, a woman who was so miserable that she overdosed on sleeping pills probably isn't the best role model. Beware of women who live by the quotes of other unhappy women.)

The Tinderella is often raised by her own version of Cinderella's evil step mother, another narcissistic woman who spoiled her daughter rotten and taught her how to manipulate and trick men for short term gain instead of how to be a good wife and mother for long-term happiness and success. So, the Tinderella may not have had a good father figure herself because her mother never settled down with one.

You should also remember in many versions of the Cinderella story the evil stepmother is responsible for the death of Cinderella's father and in our case, it could be a metaphorical death of the happiness of the men the Tinderella is involved with. The Tinderella's concept of what qualities make a "good man" are mostly centered entirely around what material things she can gain from a man in the immediate present, and she is not very interested in having a partnership focused on long term happiness together as a couple. She may be overly fixated on his physical attractiveness even if she herself is not the most attractive woman, because she is so self-conscious that she feels she must reaffirm her beauty by having a man who makes other women envious. Tinderellas typically choose men based on how much other women want them and are easily made jealous if another woman dates her ex; some part of their ego makes them believe they can always come back and get a guy they left later because they believe he "will always be there for me", and they lose self-confidence if that turns out to not be the case. This will typically make them desperate to reclaim that man's attention but if they should succeed in doing so they lose this drive, having satisfied their ego and regained their self-confidence. This is part of what makes the Tinderella such a conceited person, as their vanity is driven by how they believe others perceive them; both men and women. Without other women envious of them and without men to chase them, they lose confidence in themselves and become unstable, typically sinking into a deep depression. This drives them to engage in very toxic, self-destructive behaviors in an effort to engineer envy and desire for themselves in others.

The Tinderella may cohabitate with a man as his girlfriend for financial reasons (sometimes not paying any rent at all) but is always looking for someone else who can provide more for her, and will look to dump him if she does not get her way all of the time; and she tends to be overly demanding. To achieve this she will date and sleep with men behind his back while trying to find another man to move in with, and this can result in her passing on sexually transmitted diseases unknowingly to the man who thinks he is in a committed relationship with her.

The Tinderella is unsuitable as a mate because she has few qualities that will make her a good mother. She is too quick to anger and may even resort to violence against her own children that simply inconvenience her too much by existing at all. She lies to her man and teaches her children to lie to him on her behalf, too. The children develop major psychological issues when raised by a Tinderella for a mother and which the father may be unable to ever prevent since the courts nearly always side with the mother in custody disputes regardless of whether the mother is actually suited for motherhood or not. And so the Tinderella tends to raise her daughter to be a Tinderella, too. Her sons may grow up to have a warped perspective of normal healthy relationships and no real idea how to identify these bad qualities in other women; he may unknowingly seek out a Tinderella in his adult relationships out of a subconscious desire to "save her", as they remind him of his own mother. These efforts almost never succeed because the Tinderella does not wish to be 'saved' and feels she is succeeding at life due to the attention and gifts she receives from male suitors, even though this will eventually end after she reaches 'the wall' after menopause and loses much of her value in the dating pool (among the pool of men who wish to marry, even men who already have children with an ex-wife tend to want a new wife who can bear more children).

Consequently, the Tinderella is to be avoided in dating and when you discover you are dating one, you should discontinue the relationship as it will only lead to heartbreak and disappointment for you. The Tinderella is excellent at making a man miserable for the rest of his life if she is permitted to do so.

In my opinion most "dating advice" columns on blogs these days are written by Tinderellas who are fixated on convincing men to not date better women because they are trying to reduce the competition. They play mental gymnastics games to convince men that their bad qualities are just "independence" or "confidence" and other bullshit, and tear down actual good women who would make much better wives and mothers than themselves who possess more traditional values. Like all narcissists they develop unreasonable hatred for women with qualities they refuse to develop and they trash talk men with more traditional values who reject them as mates, even though these values are 'traditional' because they tend to result in stable, happy lifelong marriages.

Cinderella qualities

The Cinderella is the opposite of the Tinderella. She is hard working and able to handle difficult situations with grace. She is healthy and takes effort to moderate herself so as to not overly indulge into decadence. The Cinderella may not be the most successful or beautiful woman among the pool of women you can date, but she can rise to the occasion when required to. She may not always be happy, but she is often very pleasant to be around and can be a pillar of support in challenging times. She believes in reciprocating loyalty and is a 'ride or die' chick to her gentleman. She invests into a relationship with others as much as she takes from that relationship; sometimes she even invests more than what she is getting from it.

The Cinderella values the quality of a relationship, not the quantity of them she can have. If she moves in with you then she naturally desires to assume responsibility over some part of the household and contribute to it, and if she feels she cannot contribute financially as much as you she might seek to balance the scales by taking on chores such as cleaning and cooking in order to demonstrate her value as a life partner to you. The Cinderella also desires to have children and wants them to succeed in life, and will make necessary sacrifices for her children in order to improve their chances at obtaining this success. This is one of the qualities that makes her a good parent. She does not strive to live vicariously through others as she has an accurate assessment of her own self worth and possesses self-respect. She also has a personality type that can find joy even in the mundane.

Children are an important topic. Many relationship advice blogs that seek to describe ideal female qualities often become fixated entirely on personality qualities but it is important to be practical. We have to consider science, too. The reality is that the natural purpose of human romantic relationships is to have a family. I mean, if humans don't have children there will be no humans left. And while many male dating gurus these days advocate for being fatherless, I will not. If the most intelligent and financially successful men of a generation don't have children then the next generations will consist entirely of imbeciles. Watch the 2006 film Idiocracy if you want a peak at what that future will be like.

Instead, I will encourage you to date women who fit certain biological qualities, and who will make good wives and mothers given their personalities.

Many men believe because they are healthy that means their children automatically will be as well. Male sperm quality changes throughout our lives, with any recent beneficial or negative mutations we develop having the potential to be passed on. This is not the case with women, who are born with all of the eggs they will ever have. The genetic quality of their eggs is determined at birth, based on the qualities of their parents. What women do pass on is mitochondria and immune systems to their children, and any such mutations. For example, from my mother's side of the family I have inherited a rare genetic mutation that gives resistance to polio, and also provides me with a high resistance to other diseases such as HIV. I am unlikely to pass this beneficial mutation onto my own children though.

A woman's health quality can however impact the development of a fetus from the genetic instructions contained in the sperm and egg. Poor quality nutrition the pregnant mother consumes will impact the health of the child, as will engaging in practices such as smoking tobacco, drinking alcohol and other drug abuses. A woman who is overly obese prior to her pregnancy will also negatively impact the baby due to high cholesterol and blood sugar levels. All of these things greatly increase the chance of the child incubated in her womb to develop significant development disabilities as instructions on how to assemble the baby are misread.

Ideally for a wife you intend to have children with, as far as physical qualities go you want a woman who is below the age of 40, who is not obese, who does not smoke, is only a social drinker and does not engage in any kind of recreational drug usage. You also want a woman who does not have a significant medical illness which she has a high chance of passing on to the child. The purpose of having children is to pass on your bloodline to future generations, and this cannot be done if the child is sickly and dies early; or worse, struggles their entire life to achieve much of anything because of significant disorders that limit the quality of their lives. While it is impossible to completely avoid all potential problems during the fetus development, by selecting a good mate you greatly increase the chances of having healthy offspring. Intentionally choosing a mate that is in poor health greatly increases the chances of not, and often will result 100% in a child with significant developmental disabilities and which you will have to take care of for the rest of your life until they or you die — and whom will probably never have any children of their own to pass on your family legacy. Be mindful of this.

It may sound harsh and unsettling to many women to hear a man speak so bluntly about the realities of selecting a mate for marriage and family rearing, but if your goal as a man is to have healthy children then you should avoid procreating with unhealthy women. But if you absolutely feel that you must have children with a woman who is unhealthy because you love her so dearly, there are some ways to improve the situation but they are costly. You can use artificial insemination, where eggs are fertilized and screened for health problems before being inserted into the mother's womb. However, you should be aware that children produced this way have a higher than average chance of developmental problems, even if both parents are considered 'healthy'. This is believed to be because most women having the procedure are over the age of 40, which as we previously said greatly increases the chances of developmental disorders in the child. A younger mother may have a lower chance, but this is not a fully understood process.

Not being healthy is something a woman often cannot control, so it would be incorrect to call all unhealthy women a Tinderella. A Tinderella's unfitness for marriage and motherhood is a result of choices she makes, not a consequence of circumstances. Yet all the same an unhealthy woman is not a Cinderella by the definition I am promoting here, as a Cinderella is the ideal woman for a man to marry and have children with.

It may take you a long time to find your Cinderella. You may find that much like the prince in the fairy tale that you encounter her when you least expect it and that she may not stick around while you question whether to date her or not. You should never miss your chance to try to win the heart of a Cinderella for they are a rare breed of a woman; one that is becoming ever so more difficult to locate among the current generation of women today who are encouraged to become Tinderellas by bad relationship advice blogs.

The Tinderellas of today will inevitably discover too late in life that after their beauty fades they struggle to find a loyal partner to spend their remaining years with and will be miserable as they are taken advantage of in nursing homes. Even should the woman find some success on her own, without having a loyal partner she is very likely to be taken advantage of by her own bitter children or distant relatives who gain power of attorney over her affairs after something like a stroke. They then proceed to steal her life savings while sticking her in a nursing home for the last twenty or thirty years of her life. This is happening so frequently to the unmarried elderly in our society that it has pretty much become a cliché. This is also the same fate as for the so-called 'red pilled' men who prefer to live like a perpetual Peter Pan and neglect fatherhood duties. If you wish to avoid that outcome for your own life, take what I am saying here to heart.

The Cinderella is a woman of value and she knows she has it. As such she won't wait around on a man who isn't able to recognize her valuable qualities while messing around with Tinderellas. Much like a high-quality gentleman the Cinderella values her time and will move on to dating others if you take too long to realize her value to you as a mate. Unlike the Tinderella she won't do this behind your back, but she will move on from you if you take too long to decide.

When the slipper fits and you find yourself dating a Cinderella, don't hesitate to lock her down. You may never find another Cinderella again if you don't.

How to Avoid Becoming Easily Manipulated by the Media

This essay on media manipulation is designed to help men understand when creators of printed, audio and video media are trying to manipulate you with styles of persuasive writing and video editing. This is a vital skill needed to thrive in the current socio-political landscape, as if you do not know how to recognize when journalists, book authors and even just random people on Twitter, Facebook, reddit, etc. are seeking to manipulate you with these kinds of tactics.

Last year in 2020 was an election year, so we saw a lot of this kind of yellow journalism in the media, and it's only likely to keep getting worse until enough people can recognize these actions and boycott media companies that utilize these techniques designed to manipulate them into making choices against their own interests.

At its root level, manipulation in the media is achieved the same way that a stage magician manipulates the viewer; by drawing their attention to something the magician wants you to focus on while distracting you from what they are actually doing that would expose the truth.

The Role of Media in Social Manipulation

Social media frequently is designed to manipulate your emotions. Typically, non-profits are used by manipulators to shield the actual corporations that are engaging in manipulation, since being perceived as a non-profit company has a social clout image associated with it. Most people mistakenly believing that non-profits are 100% volunteer operations when in reality non-profit executives tend to be among some of the most highly paid execs in the world and usually are specialists in PR. Many non-profits are really just a type of PR company that uses its money to hire contractors to make token efforts to fulfill its mission, while pocketing the rest as salaries for employees.

As an example, in Austin, Texas there is a nonprofit that spent $18M to build 180 so-called "tiny homes" but in my opinion are really just cheaply made huts. Tiny homes, while trendy, are basically built like sheds and in fact many tiny homes began as the same models of sheds you can buy at Home Depot. These are not the same quality of materials as those used to manufacture a home and tend to be built like travel trailers, which can also have very shoddy craftsmanship to them which is why they rapidly lose value over time.

Now the local Austin newspapers tend to consider this non-profit a darling, and always positively talk about them. They launched several years ago with 180 homes, and presently after several more years they have increased to a total of 200 homes. Yet if you do the math of what the non-profit has spent into development you get a cost of $100K to make each one bedroom "house". This is ridiculous, as there are actual real houses you can buy in the area that cost $100K which have multiple bedrooms. In fact, I owned a 4 bedroom two bath, 2 story home just outside of Austin city limits a few years back, and it cost me $105K to purchase it (I sold it for about $110K when I moved). So, during the same time frame they built these ridiculously expensive "tiny homes", that money could have instead been spent to purchase existing high-quality homes. But it wasn't because the objective wasn't to provide good housing to the homeliness; the objective was to do a land development deal.

Now some people might point out they likely did not spend $100K into construction costs of each home, but this is only something those with little understanding of business costs would think. The salary costs of employees necessary to manufacture a unit should always be calculated into the final cost to build that product — in this case, the product is the tiny homes so it's more than just the cost of materials, land, permits, etc. — it's even the cost of laborers and part of that labor is above the line personnel, such as the managers of the nonprofit and the salaries they received for their time running the non-profit. This is why the cost is $100K per home, because they spent $18M and got 180 homes. So, this nonprofit is merely a grossly over-priced land development deal that price gouged using homelessness as a ploy to get people to ignore the facts of what their deal actually is; which is pretty much what every nonprofit in the country that claims to be working toward "solving homelessness" is doing. They try to "solve" homelessness by price gouging housing and charging donors — usually via state and city grants. So basically, the tax payers are being ripped off, city managers are mismanaging funds and the local media assists by never bothering to look at what the deal actually is.

Also, the problems that lead to homelessness isn't a lack of cheap housing; the actual problem is drug addictions and mental illness. Many corporations want people to think cheap housing is the reason so that they will fall for these fraudulent cheap housing scams when in reality the housing they build is not cheap, it's just shitty.

There is somewhere around 25,000 homeless people in Austin at the time I write this essay. That means it would cost $2,500,000,000 to give them each a hut — and even this won't actually solve homelessness because the underlying behavioral reasons why they are homeless are not resolved. These people aren't mentally stable enough to maintain employment in the first place, that's why they end up on the streets. So, to call this housing deals "scalable" is abuse of the English language. These are just land development deals exploiting social issues for the developers to make a buck. Also, homelessness in Austin has risen as well and violent crime even rose 23%. If homelessness in Austin continues to scale as it has been doing, there will be 2,500 new homeless people in Austin every year. So, an ongoing cost of $250,000,000 per year to give them each a space they cannot actually afford since they cannot maintain employment since their problem is drugs and mental illness.

The most popular form of non-profit that uses these tactics is the 'think tank', which do '"research" to advance certain ideas. They are predominantly funded by exceptionally wealthy families to convince politicians and the general public of supporting issues that serve the financial interests of the 'donators', who actually see their donations as an extension of public relations for their private business dealings.

How Media Uses Language to Manipulate Viewers

Journalists frequently play semantical games in an effort to manipulate the public.

Here is an example from a *New York Times* article, whose headline of the article read, *Judge Dismisses Third Degree Murder Charge in George Floyd Killing.*

The headline implies that the Judge is dismissing murder charges against the officer involved in the case, when in reality the more serious 2nd degree murder charge remained. It is expected the judge would discharge the 3rd degree charge if the 2nd degree charge was accepted.

The manipulative tactic here I am showing an example of, is that the actual event in the story are the charges the judge did not toss out, not the one that was dismissed. The more serious 2nd degree murder charges remained and only the 3rd degree one was dropped. 2nd degree murder is a more serious charge where intentional recklessness led to the death of someone, whereas 3rd degree murder is an accidental death. Yet, the writer of the *NYT* article, John Ismay, has reversed the importance of the events and made the dropping of a lesser charge the newsworthy event that he wants people to focus on, as he knows the idea of the charges being dismissed will outrage people. So he writes about what was dropped and omits what was retained to give the appearance that all charges were dismissed. The only way you'd know otherwise is by clicking out of Facebook, Twitter, reddit, etc. to read the actual article — which to be frank, many people do not do.

I have mentioned before ways that journalists engage in yellow journalism to get clicks and mislead people. Here I provided an example from *The New York Times*, but *CNN*, *ABC*, *NBC* etc. all of them do this if you pay attention.

In fact, both *CNN* and *Fox News* had similar headlines for their articles covering this incident until they edited them to be more accurate, but the *NYT* is still using the disingenuous manipulative headline to this day that I write this essay.

A statement can be technically true but also disingenuous based on what info it omits when that omission is intentional to distort the event. This is a common tactic of manipulation of information.

The headline of the *NYT* article is yellow journalism because it is designed to evoke an emotional reaction based on the implication the charges were dismissed against him; in fact, as the contents of the new article explain, the majority of charges were not dismissed, and he was still charged with second degree murder charges. It is also routine for prosecutors to bring multiple charges on principle, and for judges to dismiss the charges which have little supporting evidence for making a conviction. It isn't unusual for 3rd degree murder to be tossed out if you're also trying to convict someone of 1st or 2nd degree murder. You can't really have it both ways.

And what was the consequence of this manipulation? Well, people rioted under the belief that the "charges were dismissed". They didn't read the entire articles, they only focused on the headlines. This is why it's a disingenuous tactic for journalists to lead a story with a misleading headline. They lead with charges that were dropped, and not the more serious charges that were retained. The news article should actually have been focused on the remaining charges, not the ones that were dismissed. This is textbook sensationalism and it resulted in misleading many people into burning down their own city in outrage. Then the *NYT* had the gull to write an article about "why Minneapolis was burned down", citing frustration of the masses. This frustration was created by the *NYT* to begin with via its intentional manipulation of the facts for sensationalism. The *NYT* then further profited with more sensational articles covering all of the riots in Minneapolis and elsewhere; all a consequence of misleading the public about what was actually taking place in the criminal case.

Another tactic media companies use is the creation of infographics that are designed to lend credibility to their claims but in truth are completely meaningless. An example is the 'media bias chart' designed to convince viewers to trust some sources of information while not trusting others. This video breaks down why the entire concept is fallacious and designed to manipulate people.

More examples of the manipulation of language to lie to the public can be found by reading, *Slanted: How the News Media Taught Us to Love Censorship and Hate Journalism*.by Sheryll Attkisson. I encourage you to read it.

It will take more people recognizing that media companies often are driven to manipulate the masses to service political agendas and to cease their patronage of publications with long track records of deception in order for companies to finally cease this behavior. So long as they continue to profit from manipulation they will continue to do it.

Advice for Participating in Drinking Culture as an Adult

(This essay is for men who are of legal drinking age.)

Following the unwritten rules of society's drinking culture is necessary to navigate early adulthood without embarrassing yourself, or worse. As a young man attending film school in Ann Arbor, Michigan I personally witnessed a very drunk girl step out in front of a car after leaving a fraternity party, and I am fairly certain that she did not survive the accident. Sadly, many young people today do not get introduced to responsible drinking culture when they are still in their parents' nests, as their parents do not know what responsible drinking is, either. Yet responsible drinking is a very important skill-set for an adult, as drinking culture is deeply intertwined with social structures in universities and even in the business world; if you do not drink with some people they will assume you are not trustworthy, and people will sometimes judge the reliability and professionalism of an individual by how they conduct themselves while intoxicated at networking events. It is also worth saying that many women will judge a man based on his choice of drink and how well he handles it.

Therefore, understanding how to correctly participate in drinking culture is a necessary life skill for a gentleman and if you fail to learn it, you could make bad choices that lead to your own death.

A gentleman should strive to not consume so much spirits that he becomes a liability for others, and must be taken care of. Should you make the mistake of over-estimating how much you can drink you should strive to take care of yourself, not becoming a burden for other people. If you must spend the night sleeping on the bathroom floor by the toilet and puking as needed, that is what you must do to avoid causing issues for others due to your own error of judgement.

Why is Drinking Culture Important?

Alcohol is an essential aspect of numerous cultures all over the world. Alcohol is a part of many activities including celebrations, weddings, mourning and graduations.

Drinking culture is social behavior and traditions regarding alcoholic beverages such as wine or cocktails exist in among all ethnic groups; many of which are ancient practices. In modern society drinking culture is often called responsible drinking. Alcoholic drinks are typically casually consumed in a social setting without the intention of becoming intoxicated. Within polite society offering a drink to someone is considered a sign of friendship, gratitude or goodwill.

As many aspects of human culture revolve around the consumption of alcoholic beverages it is important for a young man to learn the unwritten rules of drinking culture so as to best navigate through social events he wishes to be a success at.

You Will be Perceived by Others Based on What You Drink

A drink is not simply done for pleasure; it is also a means of personality expression. The cocktail that you drink tells others what brand of pleasure (sometimes even punishment) you enjoy. For example, a man who drinks a bourbon-based cocktail such as an Old Fashioned or a Whisky Sour is viewed as a down to earth working man, whereas a man that frequently drinks Long Island Iced Tea or a Sex on the Beach cocktail is viewed as more feminine, as these are drinks frequently associated with frat girls. People who drink tequila or rum based drinks are often viewed as socialites, as these tend to be party drinks associated with vacationing in tropical locales. Wine drinkers, as well as those who partake of martinis, are viewed as more intellectual and sophisticated. Those who drink rarer spirits such as the green fairy absinthe are labeled as adventurous.

It should also be pointed out that certain spirits and wines better match certain kinds of foods; for example, red wine and bourbons pair very well with steaks whereas tequila and sake go well with fish. Different kinds of beers also impact the taste of food as well. Using the correct spirit for the kind of meal you are having will greatly enhance the taste of it. Those who do not partake of alcoholic drinks may feel more moral for not doing so, however they are greatly missing out on the full cuisine experience that constitutes what fine dining is. It is better to not refrain from drinking and instead simply learn how to drink in moderation; this merely requires will power.

It should be said that you should of course drink something that you want to enjoy but harder liquors take time to develop a taste for. When I first started drinking whisky it took enduring a good few weeks of punishment for my tongue to accumulate to the taste of it, and I had the same experience with red wines. If you wish to use what you drink to say something about your personality it can take effort to accumulate your tongue to the brand of alcohol you wish to be known for if you are not naturally predisposed for it.

Responsible Drinking Rules for Bars and Pubs

Drinking responsibly is an important and simple concept requiring both self-control and restraint. The issue is many individuals lose their restraint after one or two drinks, often because they drink it as if it was water and do not pace themselves. There are steps you can take to drink responsibly while protecting your health and wellbeing. You should not start drinking on an empty stomach because you will have more difficulty absorbing the alcohol properly and it will overwhelm your bloodstream, leading to early drunkenness. You should also be aware of your limit and know when to stop drinking.

By following the tips below you can avoid embarrassment and a hangover the next morning.

Know What You are Drinking

If you are served a cocktail you have never had before, ask what ingredients are in your drink. No matter how delicious or sweet your cocktail, the potency can be extremely high. Consuming only one or two drinks in a period of 15 to 20 minutes can leave you drunk. You should always be aware of the alcohol content before you drink anything so you can pace your consumption. You can easily find out simply by asking.

Drinking on an Empty Stomach

You should not go to a bar, pub or party for cocktail drinking unless you have something to eat first. In many cases you may not know if any food will be available at the party you are attending, so it can be a good idea to at least have something in your belly before attending. Your body can absorb alcohol much easier after you have consumed protein and carbohydrates which means a nice cut of beef such as from a steak is a good counter to early drunkenness. Having some meat in you will slow down the effect of the alcohol in your bloodstream. Many sophisticated drinkers will have a meal before having a single drink and there is a reason almost every pub has a healthy sized burger on the menu.

Avoiding Caffeine-based Cocktails

Alcohol can make you feel tired and exhausted. One of the worst mistakes you can make while drinking is to have an energy drink or a cup of coffee in an attempt to counter the effect of feeling intoxicated. These two things will combine their effects on you, resulting in a massive energy burst leaving you feeling jittery and shaky, unbalancing you and ultimately just making you feel more sick later. Eventually, your body will crash which is a terrible way to end an evening.

If you absolutely must combine the two, do it toward the end of the evening as a single drink to end the gathering among friends. A Jägerbomb is no way to start the night but a good way to end it.

Understanding Your Limits

Always be aware of your limits. Hard alcohol will affect you more than beer. To ensure you drink safely and responsibly, knowing your limit is critical. If you experience any adverse effects including dizziness, slurring your words or blurry vision, stop drinking immediately.

You should also be mindful of your date's limits as well. A gentleman shouldn't allow a woman to over-indulge herself and don't be too shy to ask her if she'd like to slow down. I once went on a date with a gorgeous girl who was so nervously trying to impress me that she drank an entire bottle of wine by herself trying to keep up with me. She puked all over her nice dress while I drove her back home. That was the end of the evening and a real misfortune, as she was so embarrassed we never had a second date.

Drinking and Driving

Drinking and driving is never okay in any circumstances. Choose another option such as asking a friend for a ride or calling a cab. Even if you do not feel drunk, your reactions are slower after you have been drinking. Worse, if for any reason you ever get pulled over by a cop after having a drink for something silly — like a burned out tail light on your car — the cop might make you do a sobriety test if it's late at night as a matter of course. And if you've had any alcohol in the past hour you'll likely fail that test even if you aren't legally drunk. It's best to not take any chances.

If you know you are going for a night on the town it's best to leave your car at home and get an Uber, Lyft or a taxi. You'll have a less stressful evening this way, too.

Mixing Different Alcohols

A few years back I had a ball with some pals downing Irish Car Bombs and doing tequila shots in a cozy bar in Hollywood. Typically, I hold my liquor well and don't have issues mixing alcohol but then I spotted a bottle of imported absinthe. I happen to love absinthe and decided I needed some of the green fairy to cap the night off. Boy was that a mistake! I ended that night sleeping within arms reach of the toilet on my bathroom floor.

Mixing different alcohols is a very bad idea. To avoid embarrassing yourself you should decide no more than two types of alcohol you'll be partaking of then stick with it for that evening. Drinking a glass of wine, then a screwdriver and a shot of tequila will have an adverse effect on most people's bodies.

Remain Hydrated

Alcohol draws out minerals and vitamins from your body leaving you dehydrated. You should consume a glass of water after every two or three alcoholic drinks. This will decrease your body's susceptibility to dehydration.

Among some social circles a cocktail like a screwdriver or a tequila sunrise can be viewed as a feminine drink as they contain juice, but juice-based drinks are useful and practical as they host a good amount of water content. The water helps keep you hydrated, allowing you to drink longer. I'll often consume nothing but screwdrivers at a party so that I can be social much longer, as I can drink screwdriver after screwdriver all day long and never actually get too deeply intoxicated. This is very useful when attending any kind of networking event, or a long party such as a wedding.

Pacing Yourself

Don't be a fish; avoid consuming your alcoholic beverages too fast. If you are drinking more than one alcoholic drink every hour, have something non-alcoholic in between. Too heavy of alcohol consumption will have an adverse effect on you and lead to early drunkenness and cut your evening off.

Be Aware of Your Hands

If you are attending a party or gathering where you only know one or two people, you may have a tendency to fidget with your hands. Drinking just to give your hands something to do is a bad idea. If you are feeling uncomfortable or restless, take a walk, have something to eat or hold onto a glass of water to slow down your consumption and relax.

What About Drinking Games?

Drinking games such as Kings Cup, Flip Cup and Thumper are often included at parties and social gatherings.
While these games can be enjoyable, these types of games are not considered socially responsible in more formal settings such as a networking event, because the participants of these games often become deeply drunk and too excitable. A better and more acceptable option for adding spice to a more formal party or gathering is including music, finger foods and good conversation.

Advice for Dealing with the Death of Loved Ones

For children when a loved one dies in their life, such as another parent like your wife (which sadly is not uncommon) it may be tempting to let the child withdraw from society for a time, but this is not healthy. This will teach the child to behave this way when they experience any kind of grief, and so it is an unhealthy habit to form. Ideally children first experience death with the passing of a small pet, such as a goldfish or a dog, and this first experience with losing some cherished connection with another living creature can be guided to make it easier for them to process. The burial of a pet teaches them the basics of the funeral rituals they will come to experience later in life and will need to participate in. Never shield the children from these matters and particularly cowardly children will have to be forced into attendance so that they learn to cope correctly with future tragedies and misfortunes, and the feelings of grief and loss. If you shield children from this, then they will grow up to be dysfunctional people who seek to hide from reality instead of accepting facts and moving forward in a productive way. Coddling a child from the realities of life will only produce a person who never grows up.

The best way to overcome the grief of losing a loved one is to reflect on the best of memories with that person, and what that person expected of you, if anything. All humans must someday die and be outlived by friends, family and other loved ones. This is part of the cycle of life and death that all creatures experience, but we humans are unique because we have sophisticated culture. We have language that can be used to immortalize the memory of people who once lived, allowing for proof that they once existed and the lessons that future humans can take from the life they had experienced.

To outlive the people we love is the fate of every human, just as it is to someday die. Those who outlive others have a responsibility to carry on the will of those closest to them, who entrusted a will to them. In many case, my grandparents entrusted me with their wisdom, and so I have strived to continue on with my life building upon that wisdom to become the man I am today. In the writing of this book, and my others, I pass on this wisdom that has collected inside me all of these many years. This is how I managed my grief. This is a path that others may consider in managing their own.

Recommended Reading

When I search on the internet today, I have discovered that most lists of recommended reading are useless; they are focused on promoting the latest published scribblings of people whose biographies and ideas are unworthy of the value of the paper they are printed on. You will not become educated by reading them.

What follows here is a list of books that I recommend all young men seeking to become a successful gentleman should read before their eighteen birthday. These books should fill in the gaps of knowledge that our present state of public education is failing to fill.

By reading all of these books you will gain knowledge that will help you understand the present world we live in while also bolstering your mental defenses from becoming deceived by the many charlatans that would exploit you, especially those who claim to possess special insight into history, philosophy and the sciences which they claim justifies their fraud. By reading all of these books you will become able to identify the cracks in the rhetoric of a fraudster that cause their claims to crumble. Better still if you read all of these books you will be exposed to ideas few men today are and even without a doctorate degree your peers will regard you as intelligent.

Each book in my list falls under a category and each book in each category is organized in order that I think they are best read in. To understand why you will need to read them for yourself and the process of trying to understand why I have organized them this way should assist you in your ability to digest the information.

I would like to say these are the works that I read to become the person that I am today and the precise order that I read them in, but alas, I have forgotten every book I have ever read. Rather these are books that hold certain information -- ideas -- that I think are necessary for possessing a perspective on life that is similar to my own.

Language Composition (English)

There are over 1,000 words in the English language, but most people only know the core 850 words of simplified English, which is referred to as Basic English. Organizing these words into useful sentences which can be easily understood by most people who speak English around the world is an artform. When learning other languages besides English, it is also useful to focus on the few hundred words which are most commonly used and not worry too much about the other words in the language, as this will let you converse with regular people in that language. Your speaking in the other languages will not sound pretty, but you will be able to communicate.

At any result, here are some books to assist you with mastering composition in English.

- *Self-Editing for Fiction Writers: How to Edit Yourself Into Print* by Renni Browne and Dave King
- *The Writer's Journey: Mythic Structure for Writers* by Christopher Vogler
- *Syntactic Structures* by Noam Chomsky
- *On Writing: A Memoir of the Craft* by Stephen King

History and Sociology

"Those who forget the past are condemned to repeat it."
George Santayana, philosopher

You must learn of the history of great civilizations and poor ones, for their histories are our present, and our future.

- *The Decline and Fall of the Roman Empire* by Edward Gibbon
- *The Time Traveler's Guide to Medieval England: A Handbook for Visitors to the Fourteenth Century* by Ian Mortimer
- *War and Peace and War* by Peter Turchin
- *A History of Russia, Central Asia and Mongolia*, 2 volumes, by David Christian
- *Secular Cycles* by Peter Turchin
- *Reflections on the Revolution in France* by Edmund Burke

- *The History of the United States of America During the Administrations of Thomas Jefferson and James Madison* by Henry Adams
- *Albion's Seed: Four British Folkways in America* by David Hackett Fischer
- *American Nations: A History of the Eleven Rival Regional Cultures of North America* by Colin Woodard
- *Diary of a Young Girl*, by Anne Frank
- *Kinsey Reports*, by Alfred Kinsey
- *The Origin of Species*, by Charles Darwin
- *The Descent of Man* by Charles Darwin
- *Who We Are and How We Got Here: Ancient DNA and the New Science of the Human Past* by David Reich
- *The Origin of Continents and Oceans* by Alfred Wegener
- *Our Wandering Continents* by Alex du Toit
- *The Story of Civilization*, 11 volumes, by Will and Ariel Durant
- *Atrocities: The 100 Deadliest Episodes in Human History* by Matthew White
- *Bowling Alone: The Collapse and Revival of American Community* by Robert D. Putnam
- *Necessary Illusions: Thought Control in Democratic Societies* by Noam Chomsky

Natural Sciences

Many of these are older books featuring outdated information on how the universe works. However, if you are not

300

familiar with the origin of key concepts that have contributed to our present day understanding of the universe then you cannot understand how these ideas impacted decisions of past humans. It is therefore necessary to read the original incarnation of these ideas, even if their conclusions may have recognizable errors today, to accurately understand these ideas in their proper historical context and how the sciences evolved over time into their present-day incarnations.

- *A Short History of Nearly Everything* by Bill Bryson
- *Euclid's Elements*
- *Philosophae Naturalis Principia Mathematica* by Isaac Newton
- *Essays on Philosophical Subjects* by Adam Smith
- *The Logic of Scientific Discovery* by Karl Popper
- *Experiments on Plant Hybridization* by Gregor Mendel
- *On the Origin of Species* by Charles Darwin
- *The Selfish Gene* by Richard Dawkins
- *The Meaning of Relativity* by Albert Einstein
- *The Structure of Scientific Revolutions* by Thomas Kuhn
- *Cybernetics: Or Control and Communication in the Animal and the Machine* by Norbert Wiener
- *States of Matter* by David Goodstein
- *A Brief History of Time* by Stephen Hawking

These books should be supplemented by reading encyclopedias.

Leadership Advice

These books are useful for learning the qualities that make for a good leader of men.

- *The 21 Irrefutable Laws of Leadership: Follow Them and People Will Follow You* by John C Maxwell
- *The Prince* and *The Art of War* by Niccolo Machiavelli
- *The Art of War* by Sun Tzu
- *On War* by Carl Von Clausewitz
- *How to Win Friends and Influence People* by Dale Carnegie
- *Self-Control: Its Kingship and Majesty* by William George Jordan
- *12 Rules for Life: An Antidote to Chaos* by Jordan Peterson
- *Propaganda and Persuasion* by Garth Jowett
- *War as I Knew* It by George S. Patton Jr.
- *Tribes* by Seth Godin

Philosophy

The purpose of reading these books is both to understand historical events in their correct context, as the popular philosophies of the people in history informed their choices. You also must be educated on the most popular ideologies that are present in current human societies in order to navigate your life in the most successful way. This section is not so much an endorsement of all of these ideas, but an endorsement that you must understand what these ideas are so when you encounter people who believe them you can understand what they are discussing and converse intelligently with them.

- *The Story of Philosophy: The Lives and Opinions of the Greater Philosophers* by Will Durant
- *The Republic* by Plato
- *Nicomachean Ethics* by Aristotle
- *Meditations* by Marcus Aurelius
- *Outlines of Pyrrhonism* by Sextus Empiricus
- *Enneads* by Plotinus
- *The Praise of Folly* by Erasmus
- *Novum Organum* by Francis Bacon
- *The Man in the Arena: Selected Writings of Theodore Roosevelt*
- *On the Social Contract; or, Principles of Political Right* by Jean-Jacques Rousseau
- *An Essay Concerning Human Understanding* by John Locke
- *A Treatise of Human Nature* by David Hume
- *The Rights of Man* by Thomas Paine
- *Common Sense* by Thomas Paine
- *The Federalist Papers* by Alexander Hamilton
- *Democracy in America* by Alexis de Tocqueville
- *On Liberty* by John Stewart Mill
- *Pragmatism* by Will James
- *Civil Disobedience* by Henry David Thoreau

- *Either Or* by Soren Kierkegaard
- *Brave New World Revisited* by Aldous Huxley
- *The World as Will and Idea* by Arthur Schopenhauer
- *The Abolition of Man* by C.S. Lewis
- *The Way of the Living Sword: The Secret Teachings of Yagyu Munenori*
- *Hagakure: The Book of the Samurai* by Yamamoto Tsunetomo
- *The Art of War* by Sun Tzu
- *The Analects* by Confucius
- *The Book of Five Rings*, Miyamoto Musashi
- *Summa Theologica* by Thomas Aquinas
- *Thus Spoke Zarathustra*, Nietzsche, Friedrich
- *Beyond Good and Evil*, Nietzsche, Friedrich
- *The I-Ching or Book of Changes*
- *Critique of Pure Reason* by Immanuel Kant
- *Introduction to Objectivist Epistemology* by Ayn Rand
- *Philosophical Investigations* by Ludwig Wittgenstein
- *Beyond Freedom and Dignity* by B.F. Skinner
- *Verbal Behavior* by B.F. Skinner
- *Psychology and Religion: West and East* by Carl Jung

I would also recommend you read my own work of philosophy, *The Book of Chivalric Humanism*.

Restricted Readings:

These books should only be read after all of the previously mentioned books about history and philosophy have been read, including my own works on Chivalric Humanism. The purpose of reading these restricted books is not to take to heart their lessons, for these are harmful ideologies. Rather these books should be read so that you can identify the flaws in their philosophies so you may understand why they lead to negative outcomes and caused great harm to human society. Echoes of these disruptive ideologies still permeate in human society today and it is important to understand them. Ideally, you should be at least sixteen years old when you read these books, as by this point you should have gained the knowledge and mental faculties to not be misled by them, assuming that you have read most of the other books I have included in the other lists.

There are people who say that books with harmful ideologies should be burned, but I am of the same opinion as Voltaire; if you must burn a book, it is only because you lack the wit to reply to it. Read these books, understand their arguments and in so doing, you will gain the ability to expose their weaknesses.

- *The Interpretation of Dreams* by Sigmund Freud (Highly influential on the field of psychology, although nearly everything he believed has been proven

erroneous. Must be read to understand the ideas behind pop psychology)
- *Communist Manifesto* by Karl Marx
- *Das Kapital*, by Karl Marx (these must be read to understand Marxism and how to identify it)
- *Mein Kampf* by Adolf Hitler (this must be read to understand Nazism and how to identify it)
- *Quotations from Chairman Mao Zedong*, by Mao Zedong (an imitation of Karl Marx's ideas, useful for helping to identify Communist ideologies)
- *The Course in Positive Philosophy* by August Comte (a very influential document on the field of sociology, it created the positivism movement, which became sociology. While sociology has its uses, many confuse it for a science, which it is not. Reading this will help you understand the roots of sociology and why it is not a science.)
- *Orientalism* by Edward Said (This book possesses glaring historical accuracy problems, but was influential in modern ideas that attack 'Western colonialism', mistakenly claiming colonialism is both unique to European nations and has an overwhelming negative impact in global human affairs, which is not actually the case. The book is mistaken in its conclusions but reading it is necessary to understand modern day anti-colonial ideologies as it established many of their foundational beliefs.)
- *The Vindication of the Rights of Women* by Mary Wollstonecraft (Highly influential on modern femi-

nism, this work argues that women should be educated at least for their station in life as educators, caretakers and companions of great men, which is fine. However, it must be noted Mary made poor choices in her life leading to her out of wedlock pregnancy and the subsequent economic woes. Her rebellious ideas against the cultural rules of her society without fully understanding the reasons why these rules came about almost ruined her entire life -- she attempted suicide several times -- until ironically enough she was saved from destitution by marrying a man, William Godwin. Her work should be read with the context of her life in mind to understand how her ideals betrayed her in the end.)

- *The Second Sex* by Simone de Beauvoir (This work sparked the second wave feminism movement, and inaccurately portrayed the necessary and valuable roles of women in child rearing and home making as "servitude" largely because the author did not want to be a mother and homemaker.
  - Much like with Wollstonecraft, the noble sounding ideals de Beauvoir put to paper led to a different life than she claimed it would; her open marriage influenced other feminists and notably, she and her husband Jean-Paul Sartre endorsed Marxism. Neither had any children and after a scandal in which Simone had been revealed to have started a sexual relationship with her female pupil Natalie Sorokine, she had her teaching license revoked.

Later, in 1977 she campaigned to legalize consent between minors and adults below the age of fifteen in France. Thus, de Beauvoir is not an individual worthy of emulation.

Economics

By reading these books you will gain great insight into modern economics at the global, state and personal level.

- *False Economy: A Surprising Economic History of the World* by Alan Beattie
- *The Wealth of Nations* by Adam Smith
- *The Road to Serfdom* by Friedrich Hayek
- *Law, Legislation and Liberty* by Friedrich Hayek
- *General Theory of Employment, Interest and Money*, by John Maynard Keynes
- *Omnipotent Government: The Rise of the Total State and Total War* by Ludwig von Mises
- *The Constitution of Liberty* by Friedrich A. Hayek
- *The Fatal Conceit: The Errors of Socialism* by Friedrich Hayek
- *On a Clear Day You Can See General Motors* by John DeLorean
- *Unsafe at Any Speed*, by Ralph Nader
- *Silent Spring*, by Rachel Carson
- *Empire of Pain* by Patrick Radden Keefe
- *From Mutual Aid to the Welfare State: Fraternal Societies and Social Services, 1890-1967* by David T. Beto

- *The Lean Startup* by Eric Ries
- *Blue Ocean Strategy* by W. Chan Kim and Renée Mauborgne
- *Economics of Strategy* by David Besanko, David Dranove, Scott Schaefer, and Mark Shanley.

Biographies of Great Men

Humans are capable of anything. Some represent the heights that men can reach, and others represent the depths that they can fall to.

- *The Autobiography of Benjamin Franklin*
- *How to Be Like Walt* by Pat Williams
- *The Education of Henry Adams*, by Henry Adams
- *Narrative of the Life of Frederick Douglass, an American Slave* by Frederick Douglass
- *Parallel Lives* by Plutarch
- *Theodore Roosevelt* by Edmund Morris
- *The Last Lion: Winston Spencer Churchill*, Paul Reid, William Manchester
- *Bearing the Cross: Martin Luther King Jr. and the Southern Christian Leadership Conference* by David J. Garrow

Fictional Works

- *Alice's Adventures in Wonderland* by Lewis Carrol
- *Peter Pan and Wendy* by J.M. Barrie
- *The Once and Future King* by T.H. White

- *The Hobbit* by JRR Tolkien
- *The Lion, the Witch and the Wardrobe* by C.S. Lewis
- *Red Wall* by Brian Jacques
- *Black Beauty* by Anna Sewell
- *Treasure Island* by Stevenson, Robert Louis
- *The Adventures of Huckleberry Finn* by Mark Twain
- *The Canterbury Tales* by Geoffrey Chaucer
- *The Works of William Shakespeare*
- *A Tale of Two Cities* by Charles Dickens
- *Arabian Nights*
- *Johnny Tremain* by Esther Forbes
- *Hatchet* by Gary Paulsen
- *The Lord of the Flies* by William Golding
- *Flowers for Algernon* by Daniel Keyes
- *Don Quixote* by Miguel de Cervantes
- *Ender's Game* by Orson Scott Card
- *Little Women* by Louisa May Alcott
- *Frankenstein* by Mary Shelley
- *Dracula* by Bram Stoker
- *Moby Dick* by Herman Melville
- *The Fountainhead* by Ayn Rand
- *Atlas Shrugged* by Ayn Rand
- *Nineteen Eighty Four* by George Orwell
- *Brave New World* by Aldous Huxley
- *We* by Yevgeny Zamyatin
- *The Iron Heel* by Jack London
- *Walden Two* by B.F. Skinner
- *Faust* by Johann Wolfgang von Goethe
- *The Trial* by Franz Kafka
- *The Great Gatsby* by F. Scott Fitzgerald

- *The Count of Monte Cristo* by Alexander Dumas
- *The Picture of Dorian Gray* by Oscar Wilde
- *The Call of the Wild* by Jack London
- *Fahrenheit 451* by Ray Bradbury

Myth and Legends

There are many books on myths and legends. These are a few of my favorites.

- *Grimm's Fairy Tales* by Jacob and Wilhelm Grimm
- *Le Morte de Arthur* by Thomas Malory
- *The Saga of the Volsungs*
- *The Iliad* and *The Odyssey*, by Homer
- *Bulfinchs' Mythology, Three Volumes* by Thomas Bulfinch
- *The Hero With a Thousand* Faces by Joseph Campbell

I would also recommend you read one of my prior publications, *Encyclopedia of Legendary Artifacts: The History of Mythical, Mystical and Peculiar Items from A-Z.*

Theology

You should read these, even if you are not religious or subscribe to these religions, so that you may understand the cultures of the past in their proper context, and of that which exists today that was shaped by the past. By reading these works you will better understand the major religions whose ideas shape the world today.

Some of these are very lengthy. You may not be able to complete reading them all by the time you are eighteen, when factored in with all of the other works I recommend and other education you must have. Yet, I encourage you to read some of them as your time and interest allows, so you may better understand these religions and the people whom live their lives according to their teachings.

- *The Torah* (Judaism)
- *The Christian Bible* (Christianity)
- *The Qur'an* (Islam)
- *The Ramayana* and *Mahabharata* (Hinduism)
- *Pāli Canon* and *Taishō Tripiṭaka* (Buddhism)
- *Adi Granth* and *Dasam Granth* (Sikhism)
- *Institutes of the Christian Religion* by John Calvin
- *The New Encyclopedia of the Occult* by John Michael Greer (An excellent resource for understanding the wide range of metaphysical concepts and ideas that commonly re-appear throughout human history in cults and spiritual movements).

About the Author

Carey Martell was born on December 23rd, 1982 in Newberg, Oregon. As an autodidact Carey has studied history, philosophy, sciences and other subjects mentioned in this book since he was a small boy.

When Carey was seventeen, he enlisted into the US military, first in the National Guard of Oregon in 2000, and later re-enlisting into the active component of the US Army. He served a tour of duty during Operation Iraqi Freedom from 2003 to 2004. Carey was medically discharged from the US Army in January 2005 after suffering complications from the second round of anthrax vaccine injections administrated to him.

Carey spent the next several years of his life traveling around the US, living in numerous states, and making friends and acquaintances across the country. He briefly studied in the film program of Washtenaw Community College in Ann Arbor, Michigan and then later studied film production again for a brief time at Northwest Vista in San Antonio, Texas. Carey also completed an entrepreneurial accelerator program at Tech Ranch in Austin, Texas.

Carey has founded and sold technology startups in the video streaming and new media industry, and he has also published a number of books through his imprint, Martell Books.